Activities
for a
Differentiated
Classroom

Developed by

Wendy Conklin, M.A.

SHELL EDUCATION

Consultant

Chandra C. Prough, M.S.Ed.
National Board Certified
Newport-Mesa
Unified School District

Contributing Authors

Paula Sorrell
Brenda Van Dixhorn

Publishing Credits

Dona Herweck Rice, *Editor-in-Chief*; Lee Aucoin, *Creative Director*;
Don Tran, *Print Production Manager*; Timothy J. Bradley, *Illustration Manager*;
Chris McIntyre, M.A.Ed., *Editorial Director*; Sara Johnson, M.S.Ed., *Senior Editor*;
Aubrie Nielsen, M.S., *Associate Education Editor*; Robin Erickson, *Interior Layout Designer*;
Juan Chavolla, *Production Artist*; Karen Lowe, *Illustrator*; Stephanie Reid, *Photo Editor*;
Corinne Burton, M.S.Ed., *Publisher*

Shell Education

5301 Oceanus Drive
Huntington Beach, CA 92649-1030
http://www.shelleducation.com
ISBN 978-1-4258-0732-0
© 2011 by Shell Educational Publishing, Inc.
Reprinted 2012

Table of Contents

Understanding Differentiation

As I conduct workshops with teachers of all ages and grade levels, I hear a familiar tune: *Differentiating curriculum is worrisome and stressful.* I believe this is due to the fact that teachers do not know how to begin differentiating. Their administrators tell them that they must differentiate, but teachers are overwhelmed with the task of doing it because there is not a clear explanation of what to do. Teachers know the theory. They know they need to do it. They just do not know *how* to do it.

The right way to differentiate depends on the unique students in a classroom. To successfully differentiate, teachers must first know their students. Knowing what academic level students are at helps us understand where to begin. When we have students who do not succeed, we find out why they are not succeeding. Then, we look for the type of support that they need to help them learn specific concepts. We make adjustments when students have trouble comprehending material. We look for new ways to present information, new manipulatives that make sense, and opportunities to provide additional support. As our struggling students grow, we can then scaffold the amount of support that we provide so that students continue to grow instead of leaning too heavily on that support. Differentiation is about meeting the needs of *all* students and providing the right amount of challenge for *all* students.

What Should I Differentiate and Why?

Many teachers have heard the terms *content*, *process*, and *product* when it comes to differentiating curriculum, but few have the time to ponder how these words apply to what they do in their classrooms. Below is a chart that briefly defines how we differentiate and why we differentiate.

Differentiating Curriculum

How	Why
Vary the Content (what is taught)	**Readiness** (students are not at the same academic level)
Vary the Process (how it is taught)	**Learning Styles** (students prefer different ways of learning)
Vary the Product (what students produce)	**Interests** (students have different passions)

Differentiation Strategies in This Book

What Differentiation Strategies Can I Use?

Each book in the *Activities for a Differentiated Classroom* series introduces a selection of differentiation strategies. Each lesson in this book uses one of the six differentiation strategies outlined below. The strategies are used across different curriculum areas and topics to provide you with multiple real-world examples.

Differentiation Strategy		Lessons in This Book
	Tiered Assignments	• Letters Tell About Me—*All About Me, Language Arts* • Sense Patterns—*Senses, Mathematics* • Tools in the Community—*My Community, Science* • Building Maps—*Building Things, Social Studies*
	Bloom's Taxonomy	• Popping into Descriptive Words—*Senses, Language Arts* • Shaping Up My Community—*My Community, Mathematics* • Plant Needs—*Plants, Science* • Super School Citizens—*All About Me, Social Studies*
	Multiple Intelligences	• Building Stories—*Building Things, Language Arts* • Perfect Pets—*Animals, Mathematics* • Friends Around Me—*All About Me, Science* • Sensing My World—*Senses, Social Studies*
	Choices Board	• Planting Writing Skills—*Plants, Language Arts* • Numbers All Around Me—*All About Me, Mathematics* • Amazing Animals—*Animals, Science* • Community Goods and Services—*My Community, Social Studies*
	Leveled Learning Centers	• People, Places, and Things in My Community—*My Community, Language Arts* • All Sorts of Plants—*Plants, Mathematics* • Building in Fairy Tale Land—*Building Things, Science* • Animals All Around—*Animals, Social Studies*
	Discovery Learning	• Animal Stories: Real and Fantasy—*Animals, Language Arts* • Building Towers—*Building Things, Mathematics* • Making Sense of Changes—*Senses, Science* • Plants Around the World—*Plants, Social Studies*

Differentiation Strategies in This Book (cont.)

Tiered Assignments

One way to ensure that all students in a classroom advance—using the same skills and ideas regardless of readiness levels—is to tier lessons. Often referred to as *scaffolding*, tiered assignments offer multilevel activities based on key skills at differing levels of complexity. One example of this is leveled reading texts. All students can learn about the Civil War by reading texts that are leveled according to the different reading abilities in the classroom. You can also provide comprehension questions that are leveled. Each student comes away with essential grade-appropriate skills in addition to being sufficiently challenged. The entire class works toward one goal (learning about the Civil War), but the path to that goal depends on each student's readiness level.

So, how do you tier lessons?

- **Pick the skill, concept, or strategy that needs to be learned.** For example, a key concept would be using reading skills and strategies to understand and interpret a variety of informational texts.

- **Think of an activity that teaches this skill, concept, or strategy.** For this example, you could have students summarize the information and include a main idea in the summary.

- **Assess students.** You may already have a good idea of your students' readiness levels, but you can further assess them through classroom discussions, quizzes, tests, or journal entries. These assessments can tell you if students are above grade level, on grade level, or below grade level.

- **Take another look at the activity you developed.** How complex is it? Where would it fit on a continuum scale? Is it appropriate for above-grade-level learners, on-grade-level learners, below-grade-level learners, or English language learners?

- **Modify the activity to meet the needs of the other learners in the class.** Try to get help from the specialists in your school for English language learners, special education students, and gifted learners. For this example, summarizing with a main idea would be appropriate for on-grade-level students. Above-grade-level students should include supporting details in their summaries. The below-grade-level students will need a few examples provided for their summaries. English language learners will begin with the same examples given to below-grade-level students so that they understand what is expected of them. Then, they will summarize information verbally to you.

Remember, just because students are above grade level does not mean that they should be given more work. And, just because students are below grade level does not mean that they should be given less work. Tiered lessons are differentiated by varying the *complexity*, not necessarily the *quantity* of work required for the assignment. Likewise, all tiered activities should be interesting and engaging.

Differentiation Strategies in This Book (cont.)

Bloom's Taxonomy

In 1956, educator Benjamin Bloom worked with a group of educational psychologists to classify levels of cognitive thinking. Bloom's Taxonomy has been used in classrooms for more than 40 years as a hierarchy of questions that progress from less to more complex. The progression allows teachers to identify the levels at which students are thinking. It also provides a framework for introducing a variety of questions to all students.

In the 1990s, cognitive psychologist Lorin Anderson, a former student of Benjamin Bloom, led a group of researchers to revise and update the taxonomy for the twenty-first century. There are two main changes. One involves changing the nouns to verbs. For example, instead of *comprehension* (a noun), the word is *understanding* (a verb). Also, the hierarchy of the last two levels of Bloom's Taxonomy changed from *evaluation* to *creating* as the highest form of thinking (Anderson and Krathwohl 2001).

Bloom's Taxonomy   **Bloom's Taxonomy (Revised)**

Some teachers view Bloom's Taxonomy as a ladder. They think that all students have to begin at the bottom with *remembering* questions and then progressively work their way up to the *creating* questions. It is natural for most teachers to only ask lower-level questions and assign lower-level activities. *Who is this? What is that?* Instead, this taxonomy should serve as a guide to help teachers purposefully plan for higher-order thinking. All students, regardless of readiness levels, need to develop higher-order thinking skills. At times, it is necessary to ask lower-level questions, even of above-grade-level students, when content is very new. These students typically need questions that challenge them to use higher-level thinking skills. Otherwise, they might become bored answering questions that they already understand and do not have to think about. It is just as necessary to ask below-grade-level students to evaluate a statement. However, the language of the higher-level question might need to be scaffolded for struggling students and for English language learners.

Bloom's Taxonomy is a useful model for categorizing test questions and designing lessons for your class. It differentiates the curriculum easily. Students who need background information can complete the remembering and understanding activities. Students who can access prior knowledge can do the applying or analyzing activities. Students who need a challenge can work on activities that involve evaluating and creating.

Differentiation Strategies in This Book *(cont.)*

Multiple Intelligences

The multiple-intelligences model is based on the work of Howard Gardner (1983). He has identified nine intelligences, which include verbal/linguistic, logical/mathematical, visual/spatial, bodily/kinesthetic, musical/rhythmic, interpersonal, intrapersonal, naturalist, and existential. Gardner says that everyone possesses each of these intelligences, but in each of us, some intelligences are more developed than others.

Some research suggests that certain pathways of learning are stronger at certain stages of development. Sue Teele (1994) devised a survey titled the "Teele Inventory for Multiple Intelligences." She gave it to more than 6,000 students. Her research found that verbal/linguistic intelligence is strongest in kindergarten through third grade. It declines dramatically thereafter. The logical/mathematical intelligence is strongest in first through fourth grade. It also declines dramatically thereafter. The visual/spatial and bodily/kinesthetic intelligences were shown to be dominant throughout elementary and middle school. In addition, middle-school children also show a preference for musical/rhythmic and interpersonal intelligences. Teele's findings show that if elementary teachers want to use the best strategies, they must present lessons that incorporate verbal/linguistic, logical/mathematical, visual/spatial, and bodily/kinesthetic activities.

The Nine Multiple Intelligences

- The **Verbal/Linguistic** child thinks in words. This child likes to write, read, play word games, and tell interesting stories.

- The **Logical/Mathematical** child thinks by reasoning. This child likes finding solutions to problems, solving puzzles, experimenting, and calculating.

- The **Visual/Spatial** child thinks in pictures. This child likes to draw and design.

- The **Bodily/Kinesthetic** child thinks by using the body. This child likes dancing, moving, jumping, running, and touching.

- The **Musical/Rhythmic** child thinks in melodies and rhythms. This child likes listening to music, making music, tapping to the rhythm, and singing.

- The **Interpersonal** child thinks by talking about ideas with others. This child likes organizing events, being the leader, mediating between friends, and celebrating.

- The **Intrapersonal** child keeps thoughts to him- or herself. This child likes to set goals, meditate, daydream, and be in quiet places.

- The **Naturalist** child thinks by classifying. This child likes studying anything in nature, including rocks, animals, plants, and the weather.

- The **Existential** child reflects inwardly about the ultimate issues in life while learning and interacting with others. This child likes to express opinions.

Differentiation Strategies in This Book *(cont.)*

Choices Board

Everyone loves to make his or her own choices. Getting the chance to choose what we want increases the chances that we are actually interested in what we are doing or learning. Sadly, students do not always get the chance to make choices. Curriculum plans demand that teachers teach a certain way or about a certain topic. Students have to follow along and pretend to be interested. This does not fool most teachers. One key to getting students engaged in learning is to pique their interests by offering choices. It has been noted that when students are engaged in something of interest or choice, they are more engaged in the learning process (Bess 1997; Brandt 1998). Choices can be given in a variety of ways in a classroom. Choices can be given in what students will learn (content), how they will learn (process), and how they will show what they have learned (product).

Equally important is giving students academically appropriate assignments. Tiering or leveling assignments will ensure that students work on parallel tasks designed to have varied levels of depth, complexity, and abstractness along with varied degrees of scaffolding, support, and direction, depending on each student and the topic. All students work toward one goal, concept, or outcome, but the lesson is tiered to allow for different levels of readiness and performance. As students work, they build on their prior knowledge and understanding. Tiered assignments are productive because all students work on similar tasks that provide individual challenges. Students are motivated to be successful according to their own readiness levels as well as their own learning preferences.

Choices boards combine both choices and tiering by giving students the opportunities to choose leveled activities from a larger list. The difficulty levels of the activities vary.

△ above-grade-level students (shown by a triangle)

□ on-grade-level students (shown by a square)

○ below-grade-level students (shown by a circle)

☆ English language learners (shown by a star)

There should be at least two of each leveled activity so that students have an option. A teacher controls the levels of the activities, while students control which activity they will complete within that level. For example, when giving an on-grade-level student an assignment, the teacher may tell the student to choose any square activity from the choices board, and then challenge himself or herself by choosing a triangle activity.

Leveled Learning Centers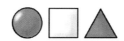

Providing academically appropriate assignments for students is important. All students need to be sufficiently challenged so that they can continue to increase their knowledge. If assignments are too easy, students will be bored and they will not learn anything new. If assignments are too difficult, students will experience stress, which can also deter the learning process.

Leveling, or tiering, assignments will ensure that all students work on parallel tasks designed to have varied levels of depth, complexity, and abstractness along with differing degrees of scaffolding, support, and direction depending on each student and the topic. All students work toward one goal, concept, or outcome, but the lesson is tiered to allow for different levels of readiness and performance. As students work, they build on their prior knowledge and understanding. Tiered assignments are productive because all students work on similar tasks that provide individual challenges. Students are motivated to be successful according to their own readiness levels as well as their own learning preferences.

When possible, teachers should also look for ways to offer students choices. When students are given a chance to choose their activities, they are likely to be more engaged in the learning process (Bess 1997; Brandt 1998).

Leveled learning centers combine the best of both worlds—choices and tiered assignments. Leveled learning centers are centers with activities that are leveled according to academic difficulty. Each student is given a choice to work at any of the centers. The following are some best practices for using leveled learning centers:

- There should be at least three centers to choose from.

- Within each center, there are activities that are appropriate for below-grade-level students, on-grade-level students, and above-grade-level students.

- The varying activity levels can be indicated by different shapes:

    △ above-grade-level activities can be identified with a triangle

    □ on-grade-level activities can be identified with a square

    ○ below-grade-level activities can be identified with a circle

    ☆ activities for English language learners can be identified with a star. These activities should contain vocabulary and language support. Partner English language learners with students who are proficient in English for additional support.

Using leveled learning centers also provides busy teachers with unique opportunities for assessment. As students work in their centers, teachers can observe students and document their progress using checklists. Teachers will be able to identify students who need more challenging activities or scaffolded work, and assignments can be quickly adjusted.

Differentiation Strategies in This Book (cont.)

Discovery Learning

Discovery learning is an inquiry-based learning method in which a teacher sets up an experiment, acts as a coach, and supports students in the process of discovering solutions.

Discovery learning is largely attributed to Jerome Bruner. During the 1960s and 1970s, Bruner worked with the National Science Foundation to develop science curriculum. Bruner believed science curriculum should help students to become problem solvers by using discovery and inquiry. As students test hypotheses and develop generalizations, they interact with the environment around them and discover solutions. When they discover their own solutions, they will better remember what was taught (Bruner 2004).

Bruner thought that science was more than merely the accumulation of wisdom from textbooks. He believed knowing was a process. When students are given structured problems, they learn concepts and problem-solving skills. The desire for knowledge motivates students to solve problems. Bruner's theory of instruction consists of the four principles below.

Curiosity and Uncertainty

The first principle of Bruner's theory is that teachers should offer experiences to make students want to learn or be predisposed to learning. The problem to be explored must offer alternative solutions. This experience must have an amount of uncertainty, which in turn would pique students' curiosity and interest in solving the problem.

Structure of Knowledge

Bruner's (2004) second (and some say most important) principle states that the teacher "must specify the ways that a body of knowledge should be structured so that it can be most readily grasped" by students. He believed that teachers could present any problem to students as long as it was simplified so students could understand it. To do this, the problem must be represented by either enactive representation (a set of actions), iconic representation (a set of pictures), or symbolic representation (logical statements).

Sequencing

Bruner's third principle states that the learner should be led sequentially through content. This will help students to understand and transfer the knowledge that is learned. First, students should complete hands-on activities that are concrete. Next, they should have a visual representation of the concept. Finally, students should move to using vocabulary or symbols having to do with the concept.

Motivation

Bruner's final principle is that rewards from the teacher should gradually decrease until students are wholly satisfied with their intrinsic abilities to solve problems. It is important for teachers to provide feedback so that students can develop confidence in their understanding.

Grouping Students

What Grouping Strategies Can I Use?

There are many variables that a teacher must consider when grouping students to create a successful learning environment. These variables include gender, chemistry between students, social maturity, academic readiness, and special needs. Some students will work well together while others will have great difficulty.

In this book, for ease of understanding, readiness levels are represented with a shape (triangle for above-grade level, square for on-grade level, and circle for below-grade level). In a classroom, however, a teacher might want to change the names for leveled groups from time to time. A teacher might use colors, animal names, or athletic team names to group students. For example, a teacher could cut out and distribute three different colors of construction paper squares, with each color representing a different readiness level. The teacher would tell all the "yellow square" students to find partners who also have a yellow square. This way, the teacher creates homogeneous groups while also allowing students to choose partners.

The following grouping strategies demonstrate various ways to group students in a differentiated classroom. This section is included so that you can learn to quickly group your students and easily apply the strategies.

Flexible Grouping

Flexible grouping means that members of a group change frequently. Routinely using the same grouping technique can lead to negative feelings, feelings of shame or a stigma associated with some group levels, lack of appropriate instruction, boredom, and behavior problems in the classroom. Flexible grouping can change the classroom environment daily, making it more interesting. It takes away the negative feelings and stigma of the struggling students because groups are always changing. No longer are the struggling students always in the same group.

Flexible grouping can occur within one lesson or over an entire unit. Try to modify groups from day to day, week to week, and unit to unit. Flexible grouping can include partner work, cooperative grouping, and whole-class grouping. Students' academic levels, interests, social chemistry, gender, or special needs can determine their placement in a particular group. Organize charts like the ones on the following pages to help you keep track of how you are grouping your students.

Grouping Students (cont.)

What Grouping Strategies Can I Use? (cont.)

Homogeneous Grouping

Homogeneous grouping brings together students who have the same readiness levels. It makes sense to group students homogeneously for reading groups and for language and mathematics skills lessons. To form groups, assess students' readiness levels in a content area. Then, order students from highest to lowest in readiness, and place them in order on a three-row horizontal grid.

One way to create homogeneous groups is by using the chart below. Notice that students in the same row have similar readiness levels.

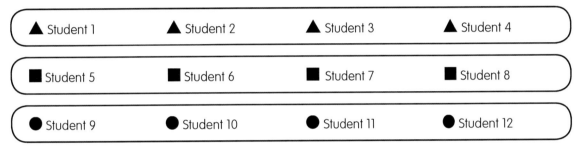

Homogeneous groups share similar readiness levels.

Heterogeneous Grouping

Heterogeneous grouping combines students with varied academic readiness levels. When grouping heterogeneously, look for some diversity in readiness and achievement levels so students can support one another as they learn together.

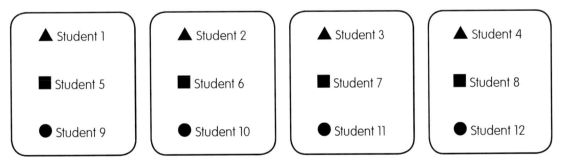

Heterogeneous groups have varying readiness levels.

Another strategy for heterogeneous grouping is to group by interest. Interest groups combine students with varied levels of achievement to create groups that have common interests. Other strategies for heterogeneous grouping include allowing students to self-select their groups, grouping by locality of seating arrangements in the classroom, and selecting groups at random.

What Grouping Strategies Can I Use? (cont.)

Flexogeneous Grouping

Flexogeneous grouping allows for the flexible grouping of homogeneous and heterogeneous groups within the same lesson. Students switch groups at least one time during the lesson to create another group. For example, the homogeneous groups meet for half the lesson and then switch to form heterogeneous groups for the rest of the lesson.

One easy flexogeneous grouping strategy is to jigsaw or mix up already established homogeneous groups. To jigsaw groups, allow homogeneous groups of students to work together for part of the lesson (circle, square, and triangle groups). Then, distinguish group members by labeling them *A*, *B*, and *C* within the same group. All of the *A*s form a new group, the *B*s form a new group, and the *C*s form a new group.

Homogeneous Groups   **Heterogeneous Groups**

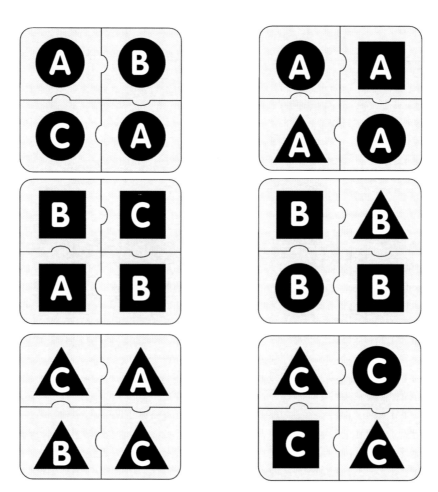

Flexogeneous grouping uses homogeneous and heterogeneous groups in a single lesson.

Working with English Language Learners

Strategies for Working with English Language Learners

Use visual media as an alternative to written responses. Have all students express their thinking through visual media, such as drawings, posters, or slide shows. This is an effective strategy for eliciting responses from English language learners. This also fosters creativity in all students, challenges above-grade-level students, provides opportunities for artistically inclined students who may struggle academically, and avoids singling out English language learners.

Frame questions to make the language accessible. At times, you will need to rephrase questions to clarify meaning for English language learners. Framing questions makes the language accessible to all students. Higher-order questions can be asked without reducing their rigor. Pose questions for English language learners with question stems or frames.

Example Question Stems/Frames

- What would happen if…?
- What is your opinion?
- Why do you think…?
- How would you prove…?
- Would it be better if…?

- How is _____ related to _____?
- If you could _____, what would you do?
- Can you invent _____?
- Why is _____ important?
- Why is _____ better than _____?

Give context to questions to enable understanding. This can be done by placing pictures or small icons directly next to key words. English language learners also benefit from chunking sentences. For example, with the question *In the ocean, how do wind and ocean currents make boats move?* English language learners can see right away that the question is about the ocean, so they have a context for answering the question.

Provide English language learners with sentence stems or frames to encourage higher-order thinking. These learners need language tools to help them express what they think. Sentence stems or frames will not only get the information you need and want from your English language learners, but it will also model how they should be speaking. You can provide these sentence stems or frames on small sticky notes for students to keep at their desks, or write them on laminated cards and distribute them to students, when necessary.

Example Sentence Stems/Frames

- This is important because…
- This is better because…
- This is similar because…
- This is different because…

- I agree with _____ because…
- I disagree with _____ because…
- I think _____ because…
- I think _____ will happen because…

Partner up, and let partners share aloud. Have English language learners work with language-proficient students to answer questions, solve problems, or create projects. Language-proficient partners can provide the academic vocabulary needed to express ideas. Prepare your language-proficient students to work with language learners by explaining that they must speak slowly and clearly and give these learners time to think and speak.

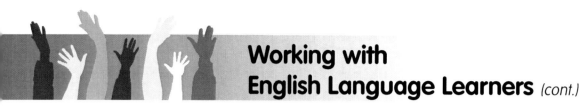

Working with English Language Learners *(cont.)*

How Can I Support English Language Learners?

All teachers should know the language-acquisition level of each of their English language learners. Knowing these levels will help to plan instruction. Using visuals to support oral and written language for students at Level 1 will help make the language more comprehensible. Students at Levels 2 and 3 benefit from pair work in speaking tasks, but they will need additional individual support during writing and reading tasks. Students at Levels 4 and 5 may still struggle with comprehending the academic language used during instruction, as well as with reading and writing. Use the chart below to plan appropriate questions and activities.

Proficiency Levels for English Language Learners—Quick Glance

Proficiency Level	Questions to Ask	Activities/Actions		
Level 1—Entering • minimal comprehension • no verbal production	• Where is…? • What is the main idea? • What examples do you see? • What are the parts of…? • What would happen if…? • What is your opinion?	• listen • point	• draw • circle	• mime
Level 2—Beginning • limited comprehension • short spoken phrases	• Can you list three…? • What facts or ideas show…? • What do the facts mean? • How is _____ related to _____? • Can you invent…? • Would it be better if…?	• move • match	• select • choose	• act/act out
Level 3—Developing • increased comprehension • simple sentences	• How did _____ happen? • Which is your best answer? • What questions would you ask about…? • Why do you think…? • If you could _____ , what would you do? • How would you prove…?	• name • label • tell/say	• list • categorize	• respond (with 1–2 words) • group
Level 4—Expanding • very good comprehension • some errors in speech	• How would you show…? • How would you summarize…? • What would result if…? • What is the relationship between…? • What is an alternative to…? • Why is this important?	• recall • compare/ contrast • describe	• retell • explain • role-play	• define • summarize • restate
Level 5—Bridging • comprehension comparable to native English speakers • speaks using complex sentences	• How would you describe…? • What is meant by…? • How would you use…? • What ideas justify…? • What is an original way to show…? • Why is it better that…?	• analyze • evaluate • create	• defend • justify • express	• complete • support

How to Use This Book

Teacher Lesson Plans

Each lesson is presented in a straightforward, step-by-step format so that teachers can easily implement it right away.

Differentiation Strategies are highlighted for quick reference.

Standards are aligned to grade-level content and English language learner needs.

Materials lists outline items needed for each lesson. If lessons call for slide show software, you might use *Microsoft Powerpoint®* or *Prezi®*. Additional resources are listed on page 167.

Preparation Notes indicate key tasks to complete prior to beginning the lesson.

English Language Support suggestions offer ideas for adapting and customizing the lesson.

Anchor Activities extend the lesson and promote further investigation and practice for students who finish early.

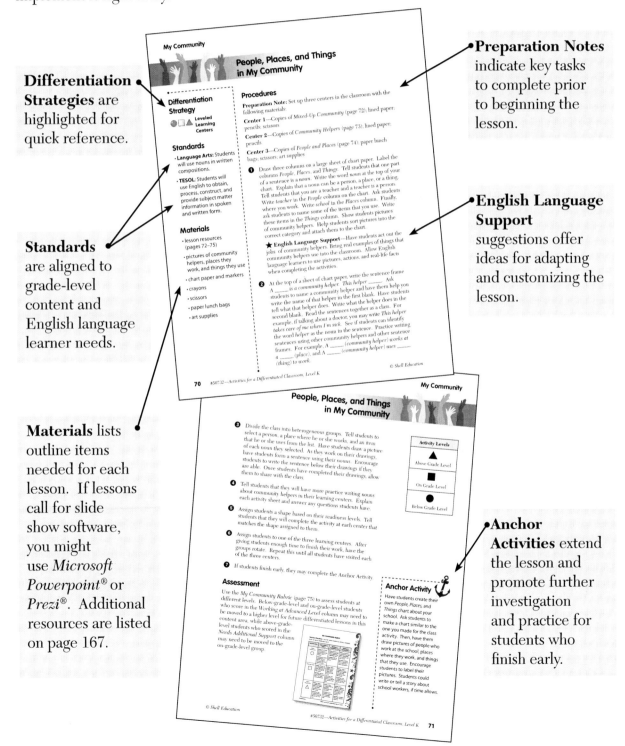

How to Use This Book (cont.)

Lesson Resources

These pages include student activity sheets and teacher resources needed to implement each lesson.

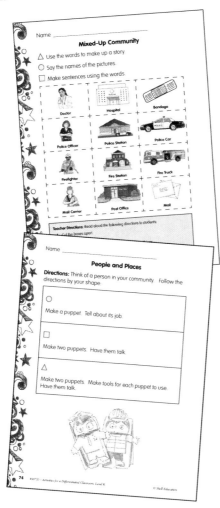

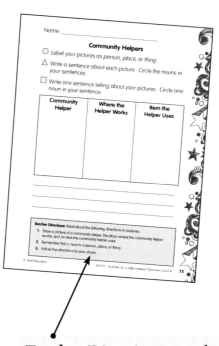

Teacher Directions provided on many activity sheets offer step-by-step instructions to read aloud to students. Additional adult support may be necessary in order for students to complete the activities.

Teacher Resource CD

Helpful reproducibles and images are provided on the accompanying CD. Find a detailed listing of the CD contents on page 168.

- Reproducible PDFs of all student activity sheets and teacher resource pages
- Reproducible PDFs of blank graphic organizers
- Answer key

Correlations to Standards

Shell Education is committed to producing educational materials that are research and standards based. In this effort, we have correlated all of our products to the academic standards of all 50 states, the District of Columbia, and the Department of Defense Dependent Schools.

How to Find Standards Correlations

To print a customized correlation report of this product for your state, visit our website at **http://www.shelleducation.com** and follow the on-screen directions. If you require assistance in printing correlation reports, please contact Customer Service at 1-877-777-3450.

Purpose and Intent of Standards

The No Child Left Behind legislation mandates that all states adopt academic standards that identify the skills students will learn in kindergarten through grade twelve. While many states had already adopted academic standards prior to NCLB, the legislation set requirements to ensure the standards were detailed and comprehensive.

Standards are designed to focus instruction and guide adoption of curricula. Standards are statements that describe the criteria necessary for students to meet specific academic goals. They define the knowledge, skills, and content students should acquire at each level. Standards are also used to develop standardized tests to evaluate students' academic progress.

Teachers are required to demonstrate how their lessons meet state standards. State standards are used in the development of all of our products, so educators can be assured they meet the academic requirements of each state.

McREL Compendium

We use the Mid-continent Research for Education and Learning (McREL) Compendium to create standards correlations. Each year, McREL analyzes state standards and revises the compendium. By following this procedure, McREL is able to produce a general compilation of national standards. Each lesson in this product is based on one or more McREL standards. The chart on page 20 lists each standard taught in this product and the page numbers for the corresponding lessons.

TESOL Standards

The lessons in this book promote English language development for English language learners. The standards listed on page 21 support the language objectives presented throughout the lessons.

Correlations to Standards (cont.)

McREL Standards	Lesson Title	Page
Language Arts		
1.6, Level I: Students will use writing and other methods to describe familiar persons, places, objects, or experiences.	Letters Tell About Me	22
	Planting Writing Skills	118
2.1, Level I: Students will use descriptive words to convey basic ideas.	Popping into Descriptive Words	46
3.3, Level I: Students will use nouns in written compositions.	People, Places, and Things in My Community	70
6.1, Level I: Students will use reading skills and strategies to understand a variety of familiar literary passages and texts (e.g., fiction, nonfiction, picture books, and predictable books).	Animal Stories: Real and Fantasy	142
6.3, Level I: Students will know the setting, main characters, main events, sequence, and problems in stories.	Building Stories	94
Mathematics		
5.5, Level Pre-K: Students will sort and group objects by attributes (e.g., shape, size, color).	All Sorts of Plants	124
2.1, Level I: Students will understand that numerals are symbols used to represent quantities or attributes of real-world objects.	Numbers All Around Me	28
3.3, Level I: Students will understand basic estimation strategies (e.g., using reference sets, using front-end digits) and terms (e.g., *about, near, closer to, between, a little less than*).	Building Towers	100
5.3, Level I: Students will know that geometric shapes are useful for representing and describing real-world situations.	Shaping Up My Community	76
6.1, Level I: Students will collect and represent information about objects or events in simple graphs.	Perfect Pets	148
8.2, Level I: Students will be able to create and extend simple patterns.	Sense Patterns	52
Science		
4.2, Level I: Students will know that differences exist among individuals.	Friends Around Me	34
5.1, Level I: Students will know the basic needs of plants.	Plant Needs	130
7.2, Level I: Students will know there are similarities and differences in the appearance and behavior of plants and animals.	Amazing Animals	154
8.1, Level I: Students will know that different objects are made up of many different types of materials and have many different observable properties.	Building in Fairy Tale Land	106
8.2, Level I: Students will know that things can be done to materials to change some of the properties (e.g., heating, freezing, mixing, cutting, dissolving, bending).	Making Sense of Changes	58
12.2, Level I: Students will know that tools (e.g., thermometers, magnifiers, rulers, balances) can be used to gather information and extend the senses.	Tools in the Community	82
Social Studies		
Behavioral Studies 3.1, Level I: Students will know that people use their senses to find out about their surroundings.	Sensing My World	64
Behavioral Studies 4.3, Level I: Students will understand that rules at home and in the community will let individuals know what to expect.	Super School Citizens	40
Economics 1.1, Level I: Students will understand that goods are objects that can satisfy people's wants and services are activities that can satisfy people's wants.	Community Goods and Services	88
Geography 4.1, Level I: Students will understand the physical and human characteristics of a place.	Building Maps	112
Geography 5.1, Level I: Students will understand that areas can be classified as regions according to physical criteria (e.g., landform regions, soil regions, vegetation regions, climate regions, water basins).	Plants Around the World	136
Social Studies 4.2, Level I: Students will know that places can be defined in terms of their predominant human and physical characteristics (e.g., forest, desert; or by types of landforms, vegetation, water bodies, climate).	Animals All Around	160

Correlations to Standards (cont.)

TESOL Standards	Lesson Title	Page
TESOL 2.2 — Students will use English to obtain, process, construct, and provide subject matter information in spoken and written form to achieve academically in all content areas.	Letters Tell About Me	22
	Numbers All Around Me	28
	Friends Around Me	34
	Super School Citizens	40
	Popping into Descriptive Words	46
	Sense Patterns	52
	Making Sense of Changes	58
	Sensing My World	64
	People, Places, and Things In My Community	70
	Shaping Up My Community	76
	Tools in the Community	82
	Community Goods and Services	88
	Building Stories	94
	Building Towers	100
	Building in Fairy Tale Land	106
	Building Maps	112
	Planting Writing Skills	118
	All Sorts of Plants	124
	Plant Needs	130
	Plants Around the World	136
	Animal Stories: Real and Fantasy	142
	Perfect Pets	148
	Amazing Animals	154
	Animals All Around	160

Letters Tell About Me

Differentiation Strategy

 Tiered Assignments

Standards

- **Language Arts:** Students will use writing and other methods to describe familiar persons, places, objects, or experiences.

- **TESOL:** Students will use English to obtain, process, construct, and provide subject matter information in spoken and written form.

Materials

- lesson resources (pages 24–27)

- paper lunch bags (one with objects that tell about you)

- alphabet chart with pictures or picture cards

- sticky notes

- large paper (12" x 18")

- scissors

- glue

- art supplies

Procedures

Preparation Note: Prepare a small paper bag by drawing a picture of yourself on the bag. Place items in the bag that begin with the same letter as your name. Select items that tell about you, if possible.

1 Show your completed bag to students. Ask them to identify the drawing on the bag. Pull items out of the bag one at a time. Have students name each object and state the beginning letter of each object. If they have difficulty, use the alphabet chart and prompting questions such as *Does it begin with* b? *Does it begin with* i? If the objects describe you, explain their significance to the class.

2 Distribute paper lunch bags to students. Have them draw their picture and write their name on the paper bag. Tell students that their job is to take the bags home and collect three or four small items that begin with the same letter as their name and then place them in the bag. Encourage students to find items that tell about them. Ask students to bring the bag back to school the next day. Distribute copies of the *Letters Tell About Me* parent letter (page 27) to students and read it aloud. Explain to students that this letter will let their parents know how to help them with the bag.

3 Once the paper bags have been returned, give each child a sticky note. Ask them to write the first letter of their name on the sticky note.

★ **English Language Support**—Allow students to work with a partner to identify objects in the classroom. Have them find something in the room that begins with their letter and attach their note to the item. Have each student share the item that he or she found by repeating the following sentence. "(Letter) is for (name of student) and (object in room)." Display this sentence frame for students to use when speaking.

4 Review the contents of your bag, displaying each item one at a time. Name each item and explain again how it tells about you. Allow students to share the contents of their bags. As each child shares, write his or her name on a large sheet of paper and list the contents of their bag. If time permits, have students draw a picture of each object on their paper. Hang the posters in the classroom in alphabetical order.

Letters Tell About Me

5 Explain to students that they will have an opportunity to learn more about letters and their names. Distribute copies of the *Letters in My Name* activity sheets (pages 24–26) to students based on their readiness level.

Activity Levels
▲
Above Grade Level
■
On Grade Level
●
Below Grade Level

6 Place students into small homogeneous groups and explain the directions for each activity sheet to the groups, beginning with the below-grade-level students. You may need to write some students' names for them. Provide students with scissors, glue, and drawing materials to help them complete the activities.

7 Once students have completed the tiered assignments, have them share their work with two other classmates. This will allow the students to get to know one another.

8 If students finish early, they may complete the Anchor Activity.

Assessment

Circulate around the room as students complete their *Letters in My Name* activity sheets. Ask questions of students to assess their understanding of the concept. Make anecdotal notes about students' ability to identify letters and write their names.

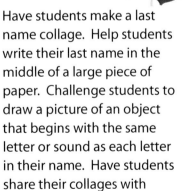

Anchor Activity

Have students make a last name collage. Help students write their last name in the middle of a large piece of paper. Challenge students to draw a picture of an object that begins with the same letter or sound as each letter in their name. Have students share their collages with a friend.

Name _____

Letters in My Name

<u>Dan</u> likes <u>dogs</u>.

_____ likes _____.

_____ likes _____.

_____ likes _____.

_____ likes _____.

Teacher Directions: Read aloud the following directions to students:

1. Think of the first letter of your name. What sound does it make? Cut out or draw pictures that begin with the same sound as the first letter of your name. Put them in the box.

2. Write sentences about things you like that start with the same letter as your first name. See the sample sentence, *Dan likes dogs.*

Name _____

Letters in My Name

_____

Teacher Directions: Read aloud the following directions to students:

1. Write your first name on the line in the box.

2. Find or draw a picture for each letter of your name. Glue them in the box.

3. Write the letter that goes with each picture next to it.

Name _____

Letters in My Name

Teacher Directions: Read aloud the following directions to students:

1. Write your first name in the box.

2. Point to each letter and say the letter out loud.

3. Draw pictures of things that begin with the first letter in your name.

#50732—*Activities for a Differentiated Classroom, Level K*   © *Shell Education*

Letters Tell About Me

Date _____

Dear Parents or Guardians,

Our class is learning about the letters in our names. Your child has drawn a picture of himself or herself on a paper lunch bag and brought it home. To fill the bag, please help your child find three or four objects at home that begin with the same letter as his or her name. Try to select objects that tell about your child, if at all possible. Be sure to label each item you place in the bag. While we will take good care of the items, please do not include items that are easily broken or sentimental. Please make sure these bags are sent to school tomorrow. The students will be sharing their bags with our class.

Sincerely,

_____

Numbers All Around Me

Differentiation Strategy

Choices Board

Standards

- **Mathematics:** Students will understand that numerals are symbols used to represent quantities or attributes of real-world objects.

- **TESOL:** Students will use English to obtain, process, construct, and provide subject matter information in spoken and written form.

Materials

- lesson resources (pages 30–33)
- number cards (1–9)
- groups of manipulatives
- chart paper and markers
- *Bar Graph* activity sheet (bargraph.pdf)
- old magazines, scissors, glue, construction paper
- scale
- snap cubes
- index cards
- pocket chart *(optional)*

Procedures

Preparation Note: Make copies of the *Numbers All Around Me Choices Cards* activity sheets (pages 31–33) and cut them apart. There is one blank shape on each of the card pages. You can insert an additional activity on those cards, if desired.

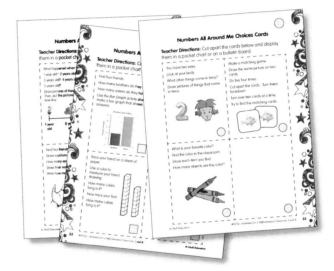

1. Show students the number cards in random order and ask them to identify the number on each card. Display a group of manipulatives, such as six blocks. Have students count the blocks as you point to each one. After counting, ask a student to find the number 6 card and place it beside the six blocks. Repeat this process with other groups of objects.

2. Tell students that you are thinking of a number (five), and you would like them to guess the number. Give clues, such as *The number is greater than three* or *The number is less than eight*. After they have guessed the number, ask students how that number describes something about them. They might give answers such as the number represents their age, their fingers on one hand, their favorite number, or the number of people in their family. List each of their ideas on a sheet of chart paper as they are named.

3. Remind students that numbers have meaning. Numbers are symbols that show the total amount. An example of this is that a certain number can tell how many people are in a family.

Numbers All Around Me

★ **English Language Support**—As you work through the lesson, hold up cards with numbers as you talk about specific numbers. Also, use visual clues, pictures, and gestures as you explain how numbers relate to specific things. Work with these learners as they complete the activities on the choices board.

Activity Levels
▲
Above Grade Level
■
On Grade Level
●
Below Grade Level

4 Have students draw pictures of the members of their families on sheets of drawing paper. Then, create a class bar graph to show the number of family members in each student's family. Use the number cards as labels for the bar graph. Discuss which students have three members, four members, and so on. See if students can identify the person in the class with the most family members and the person with the fewest family members.

5 Tell students that numbers show us information and tell us how many there are of something. Students will have an opportunity during class to practice using numbers. Assign students a shape that corresponds to their readiness levels.

6 Tell students that they will choose two activities that have the shape that you assigned them. One activity will be completed individually, and one activity will be completed with a friend who also has the same shape. Be sure to place students with friends who have similar academic readiness levels for the second activity.

7 Display the *Numbers All Around Me Choices Cards* activity sheets (pages 31–33) in a pocket chart or on a bulletin board. Read through all the activities on the choices board. Refer to the *Numbers All Around Me Choices Board* sheet (page 30) for an example of how to display the cards. Have students choose two activities that they want to complete. Give students time to complete these activities.

8 If students finish early, they may complete the Anchor Activity.

Assessment

Observe students as they work on their activities. Note which students struggle and which complete the activity with ease. Use this information to regroup students as necessary for future differentiation.

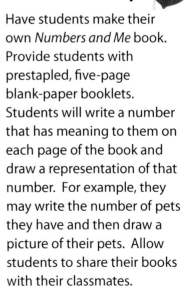

Anchor Activity

Have students make their own *Numbers and Me* book. Provide students with prestapled, five-page blank-paper booklets. Students will write a number that has meaning to them on each page of the book and draw a representation of that number. For example, they may write the number of pets they have and then draw a picture of their pets. Allow students to share their books with their classmates.

Numbers All Around Me Choices Board

Teacher Directions: Display the choices cards (pages 31–33) on a pocket chart or bulletin board as shown below:

You have two eyes. Look at your body. What other things come in twos? Draw pictures of things that come in twos. ○	Find four friends. How many brothers do they have? How many sisters do they have? Use the *Bar Graph* activity sheet to make a bar graph that shows their answers. □	What happened when you were . . . 1 year old? 2 years old? 3 years old? 4 years old? 5 years old? Draw pictures of these things. Then, put the pictures in order on a time line. △
Make a poster of things you like. Cut out pictures from magazines. Count the number of pictures on your poster. Write that number. □	Weigh yourself. Weigh a friend. Draw a picture that compares the numbers. △	Make a matching game. Draw the same picture on two cards. Do this four times. Cut apart the cards. Turn them facedown. Turn over two cards at a time. Try to find the matching cards. ○
Find four friends. Draw a picture of each of their eyes. How many eyes all together? Draw their noses, hands, and fingers. Write how many of each. △	Trace your hand on a sheet of paper. Use a cube to measure your hand drawing. How many cubes long is it? Now trace your foot. How many cubes long is it? □	What is your favorite color? Find the color in the classroom. Draw each item you find. How many objects are this color? ○

Numbers All Around Me Choices Cards

Teacher Directions: Cut apart the cards below and display them in a pocket chart or on a bulletin board.

What happened when you were . . .

1 year old? 2 years old?

3 years old? 4 years old?

5 years old?

Draw pictures of these things.
Then, put the pictures in order on a time line.

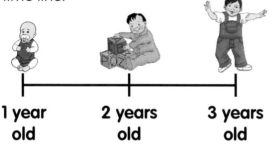

| **1 year old** | **2 years old** | **3 years old** |

Weigh yourself.

Weigh a friend.

Draw a picture that compares the numbers.

Find four friends.

Draw a picture of each of their eyes.

How many eyes all together?

Draw their noses, hands, and fingers.

Write how many of each.

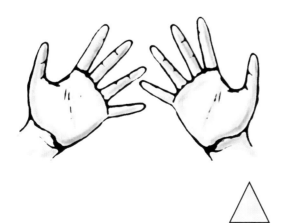

Numbers All Around Me Choices Cards

Teacher Directions: Cut apart the cards below and display them in a pocket chart or on a bulletin board.

Find four friends.

How many brothers do they have?

How many sisters do they have?

Use the *Bar Graph* activity sheet to make a bar graph that shows their answers.

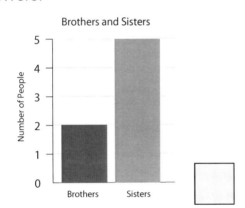

Make a poster of things you like.

Cut out pictures from magazines.

Count the number of pictures on your poster.

Write that number.

Trace your hand on a sheet of paper.

Use a cube to measure your hand drawing.

How many cubes long is it?

Now trace your foot.

How many cubes long is it?

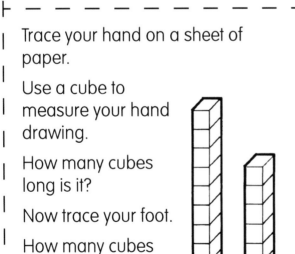

Numbers All Around Me Choices Cards

Teacher Directions: Cut apart the cards below and display them in a pocket chart or on a bulletin board.

You have two eyes.

Look at your body.

What other things come in twos?

Draw pictures of things that come in twos.

Make a matching game.

Draw the same picture on two cards.

Do this four times.

Cut apart the cards. Turn them facedown.

Turn over two cards at a time.

Try to find the matching cards.

What is your favorite color?

Find the color in the classroom.

Draw each item you find.

How many objects are this color?

Friends Around Me

Differentiation Strategy

 Multiple Intelligences

Standards

- **Science:** Students will know that differences exist among individuals.
- **TESOL:** Students will use English to obtain, process, construct, and provide subject matter information in spoken and written form.

Materials

- lesson resources (pages 36–39)
- yarn to create a Venn diagram on the floor
- index cards
- markers
- flat craft sticks, tongue depressors, or pencils
- scissors
- crayons
- glue

Procedures

❶ Make a large Venn diagram on the floor using yarn. Have two students come to the front of the class. Ask the class to name ways that students are alike and ways that they are different. Write each idea on an index card. Place the index cards in the correct location on the Venn diagram.

❷ Tell students that although both students are kindergarteners, they have characteristics that are the same and different. Explain that a *characteristic* is a feature that describes a person. Ask students if they can tell you where you placed the cards that show how these two students are the same. (*They should identify the center where the diagram overlaps.*) Have students show you where you placed the cards that show how these two students are different. (*They should be the parts of the diagram that do not overlap.*)

❸ Show students the *Friends Are the Same but Different* activity sheet (page 36). Tell students that they are going to make comparisons with a partner just as you did on the large Venn diagram. Students can write in words or draw pictures on the Venn diagram. Assign each student a partner and distribute copies of the activity sheet to each pair. Monitor students to be sure that they are placing information in the proper location on the diagram.

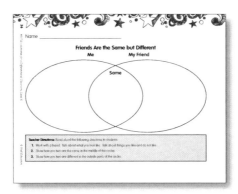

Friends Around Me

❹ When students have completed the Venn diagrams, meet as a whole class. Allow students to share some of the things that they found to be the same and different about each other.

❺ Tell students that they will have an opportunity to learn more about similarities and differences among classmates during activity time. Demonstrate and explain each activity sheet for the class. *Picture My Friends* (page 37) accesses the visual/spatial intelligence; *Act Like My Friends* (page 38) reaches the bodily/kinesthetic intelligence; and *Survey My Friends* (page 39) addresses the logical/mathematical intelligence. Tell students that they will choose which activity sheet they want to complete. Provide students with any needed materials to help them complete the activities.

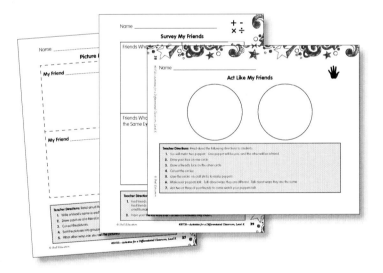

★ **English Language Support**—Allow English language learners to partner with language-proficient students as they complete the multiple intelligences activities.

❻ If students finish early, they may complete the Anchor Activity.

Assessment

Document which of the activities students choose to complete and record their levels of success on the activity. This information will assist you in determining students' strengths within the multiple intelligences and guide future differentiated assignments for each student.

Anchor Activity

Have students create a chart showing what makes them special. They should draw a detailed picture of themselves on the chart that shows correct eye, hair, and skin color. They can draw pictures of their skills, talents, and hobbies as well as their likes and dislikes. Encourage students to label their charts.

Name _____

Friends Are the Same but Different

Me   **My Friend**

Same

Teacher Directions: Read aloud the following directions to students:

1. Work with a friend. Talk about what you look like. Talk about things you like and do not like.

2. Show how you two are the same in the middle of the circles.

3. Show how you two are different in the outside parts of the circles.

Name _____

Picture My Friends

My Friend _____

My Friend _____

My Friend _____

My Friend _____

Teacher Directions: Read aloud the following directions to students:

1. Write a friend's name in each box.

2. Draw a picture of a friend in each box. Color each picture.

3. Cut out the pictures.

4. Sort the pictures into groups. You can sort by hair color or eye color.

5. What other ways can you sort the pictures?

Name _____

Act Like My Friends

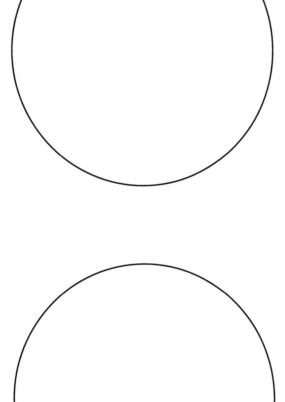

Teacher Directions: Read aloud the following directions to students:

1. You will make two puppets. One puppet will be you, and the other will be a friend.

2. Draw your face on one circle.

3. Draw a friend's face on the other circle.

4. Cut out the circles.

5. Glue the circles on craft sticks to make puppets.

6. Make your puppets talk. Talk about ways they are different. Talk about ways they are the same.

7. Ask two or three of your friends to come watch your puppets talk.

Name _____

Survey My Friends

Friends Who Are Tall 	Friends Who Have the Same Hair Color
Friends Who Have the Same Eye Color	Friends Who Have Small Hands

Teacher Directions: Read aloud the following directions to students:

1. Find friends who are tall. Find friends with the same hair color as one another. Find friends with the same eye color as one another. Find friends with small hands.

2. Have your friends write their names in the boxes they match.

Super School Citizens

Differentiated Strategy

 Bloom's Taxonomy

Standards

- **Social Studies:** Students will understand that rules at home and in the community will let individuals know what to expect.

- **TESOL:** Students will use English to obtain, process, construct, and provide subject matter information in spoken and written form.

Materials

- lesson resources (pages 42–45)

- scissors

- pictures of people and places in a community (*See page 167.*)

- chart paper and markers

- art supplies

Procedures

Preparation Note: Cut apart the activity cards on the *Super School Citizens* activity sheet (page 42).

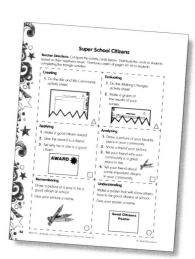

1 Tell students that they will be discussing communities and citizens. Explain that a community is made up of the people who live near one another and of the places they share. Have students name specific places in their community. They should include homes, parks, libraries, schools, hospitals, and other places found in communities. Tell students that the people who live and work in communities are called *citizens*.

★ **English Language Support**—Provide English language learners with pictures that represent *community* and *citizens*.

2 Ask students to identify an important place in their community where they spend a lot of time. Help students to name their school as that place and to identify themselves as citizens of their school. Tell students that they are citizens in both their school and their community. Have students brainstorm ways to be good citizens at school. These may include sharing, being good friends, helping others, taking care of the school, being honest, doing their best, and following rules. List the students' ideas on a sheet of chart paper.

3 Cut apart each of the good-citizen ideas you wrote on the chart. Divide students into heterogeneous groups of two or three. Give each group a piece of chart paper with a good-citizen idea listed. Have groups work together to act out a way to be a good citizen at school.

4 After each group has play-acted being good citizens at school, discuss why it is important to be a good citizen not only in school but also in the community. Discuss how the people in the community work together to make it a nice place to live.

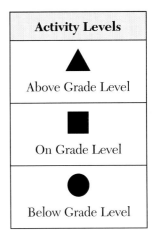

Super School Citizens

⑤ Tell students that they will have more opportunities to learn about and practice being good citizens during activity time. Distribute the activity cards from the *Super School Citizens* activity sheet (page 42) to students based on their readiness levels. Explain and demonstrate each activity. Students should complete two activities. Some of these activities require additional activity sheets. Distribute copies of the *Me and My Community* activity sheet (page 43) and the *Making Changes* activity sheet (page 44) to students who are completing the triangle activities.

Activity Levels
▲
Above Grade Level
■
On Grade Level
●
Below Grade Level

⑥ If students finish early, they may complete the Anchor Activity.

Assessment

Observe students as they work and ask questions about the meanings of *community* and *citizens*. You may wish to make a simple checklist to record students' progress toward mastery of this standard.

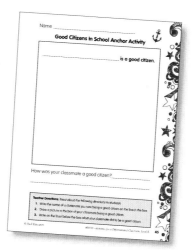

Anchor Activity ⚓

Have students write about and draw ways in which they have seen their friends being good citizens at school. Prepare copies of the *Good Citizens in School Anchor Activity* sheet (page 45). Collect each completed page and keep it in a Good Citizen Journal.

Super School Citizens

Teacher Directions: Cut apart the activity cards below. Distribute the cards to students based on their readiness levels. Distribute copies of pages 43–44 to students completing the triangle activities

Creating

1. Do the *Me and My Community* activity sheet.

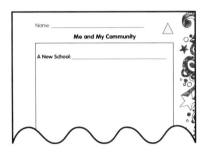

Evaluating

1. Do the *Making Changes* activity sheet.

2. Make a graph of the results of your survey.

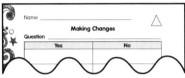

Applying

1. Make a good citizen award.
2. Give the award to a friend.
3. Tell why he or she is a good citizen.

AWARD

Analyzing

1. Draw a picture of your favorite place in your community.
2. Show a friend your picture.
3. Tell your friend why your community is a great place to live.
4. Tell your friend about some important citizens in your community.

Remembering

1. Draw a picture of a way to be a good citizen at school.
2. Give your picture a name.

Understanding

1. Make a poster that will show others how to be good citizens at school.
2. Give your poster a name.

Good Citizens Poster

Name _____

Me and My Community

A New School: _____

School Rules:

1. _____

2. _____

3. _____

Teacher Directions: Read aloud the following directions to students:

1. Draw a pretend school.

2. Give your school a name.

3. Make a list of rules in your school that good citizens must follow.

Name _____

Making Changes

Question _____

Yes	No

How many friends said *yes*? _____

How many friends said *no*? _____

Teacher Directions: Read aloud the following directions to students:

1. Think of a change you want to make in your school.

2. Write a question about the change on the line.
   Example: Do you want longer recesses?

3. Ask your friends the question. If they say *yes*, ask them to write their name in the *yes* column. If they say *no*, have them write their name in the *no* column.

Name _____

Good Citizens in School Anchor Activity

_____ **is a good citizen.**

How was your classmate a good citizen?_____

_____

Teacher Directions: Read aloud the following directions to students:

1. Write the name of a classmate you saw being a good citizen on the line in the box.

2. Draw a picture in the box of your classmate being a good citizen.

3. Write on the lines below the box what your classmate did to be a good citizen.

Popping into Descriptive Words

Differentiated Strategy

Bloom's Taxonomy

Standards

- **Language Arts:** Students will use descriptive words to convey basic ideas.

- **TESOL:** Students will use English to obtain, process, construct, and provide subject matter information in spoken and written form.

Materials

- lesson resources (pages 48–51)
- index cards
- popcorn kernels
- air popcorn popper or microwave
- bowls
- chart paper and markers
- large construction paper
- crayons
- popcorn toppings, such as salt, powdered cheese, cinnamon, chocolate, or caramel sauce

Procedures

Preparation Note: Cut apart the activity cards on the *Popping Good Words* activity sheet (page 48).

1 Play a guessing game with students. Tell them you are going to use special words called *adjectives* to describe someone. Use adjectives to describe a student. See if the students can correctly guess the person whom you are describing.

2 Describe a few more students and allow students to guess their identities. You might wish to have students provide the descriptions. Remind them that the descriptive words they are using are called *adjectives*.

★ **English Language Support**—Write a variety of adjectives on index cards that could be used to describe characteristics of people. For example, *blue* eyes, *curly* hair, *striped* shirt, and *tall* boy are descriptive. Draw a picture on each adjective card. Work with English language learners to create new adjectives based on examples that they can see in the classroom. For example, they may identify a *green* jacket, *brown* sandals, or *long* hair.

3 Place some popcorn kernels in a bowl. Allow students to look at and touch the kernels as they pass around the bowl. Ask students to describe the kernels. If possible, use an air popcorn popper to make popcorn. You can also bring in popcorn popped in a microwave.

4 List each of the five senses on a piece of chart paper (see, taste, touch, smell, and hear). Ask one student to use an adjective and describe how the popcorn looks. Write his or her word on the chart. Follow this procedure for each of the other senses.

5 Divide the class into five heterogeneous groups. Give each group a bowl of popcorn and a sheet of construction paper. Assign each group one of the five senses and have them write or draw a picture of this sense at the top of their paper. Tell students that they are to use their assigned sense to describe the popcorn. Encourage students to draw pictures and write words describing the popcorn.

Popping into Descriptive Words

6 Once students have completed the activity, gather together and allow each group to share their descriptive words. Add their words to the appropriate place on your class chart.

7 Divide the class into homogeneous groups. Assign each group a shape based on students' readiness levels.

8 Distribute the *Popping Good Words* activity cards to students based on their readiness levels. Explain the activities and demonstrate how to complete each one. Some of these activities require additional activity pages. Above-grade-level students will receive the *New Creation* activity sheet (page 49). On-grade-level students will receive the *Yummy-Yucky Chart* (page 50). Below-grade-level students will receive the *Describing Popcorn* activity sheet (page 51). Monitor students as they work on assignments and provide materials and assistance, as needed.

Activity Levels
▲
Above Grade Level
■
On Grade Level
●
Below Grade Level

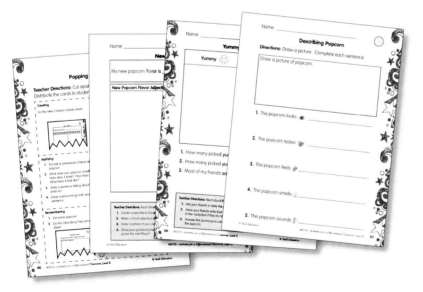

9 If students finish early, they may complete the Anchor Activity.

Assessment

Circulate around the room while students work in groups and ask questions to assess their learning. Make anecdotal notes and keep records on each student's progress.

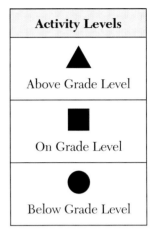

Anchor Activity

Have students draw pictures or write the name of a food they like to see, taste, touch, smell, and hear. Then, have students write adjectives or sentences about the food. Have students read the describing words to a friend and see if the friend can guess the food.

Popping Good Words

Teacher Directions: Cut apart the activity cards below. Distribute the cards to students based on their readiness levels.

Creating

Do the *New Creation* activity sheet.

Evaluating

1. What is your favorite type of popcorn?
2. Make a poster to show your friends how good this popcorn is.
3. Draw a picture for your poster.
4. Use adjectives that will make people want to try your popcorn.

Applying

1. Put salt or powdered cheese on the popcorn.
2. What does your popcorn smell like? How does it taste? How does it feel? What does it look like?
3. Write a sentence telling about the popcorn.
4. Draw a picture to go with your sentence.

Analyzing

Do the *Yummy-Yucky Chart activity sheet*.

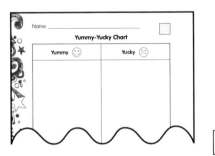

Remembering

1. Eat some popcorn.
2. Do the *Describing Popcorn* activity sheet.

Understanding

1. Write a sentence describing popcorn.
2. Use your senses to describe the popcorn.
3. Draw a picture to match your sentence.

Name _____

New Creation

My new popcorn flavor is _____.

New Popcorn Flavor Adjectives	Picture of My New Creation

Teacher Directions: Read aloud the following directions to students:

1. Create a new flavor of popcorn.

2. Make a list of adjectives describing your new popcorn.

3. Draw a picture of your popcorn.

4. Show your picture to your friends. Read aloud your adjectives. Can your friends guess the new flavor?

Name _____

Yummy-Yucky Chart

Yummy 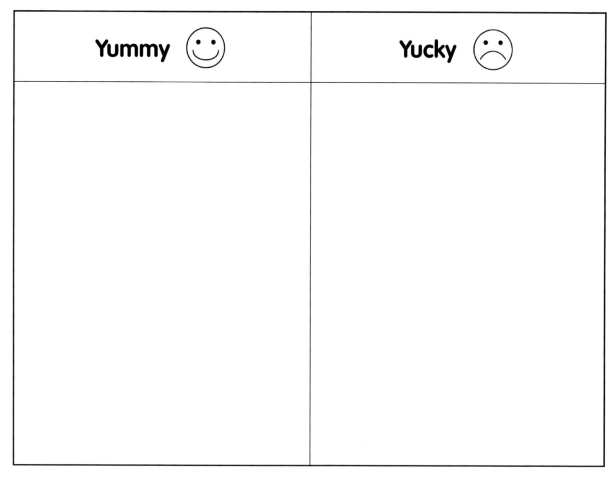	Yucky

1. How many picked *yummy* ☺? _____.

2. How many picked *yucky* ☹? _____.

3. Most of my friends said the popcorn is _____.

Teacher Directions: Read aloud the following directions to students:

1. Ask your friends to taste the popcorn.

2. Have your friends write their names in the *Yummy* box if they like the popcorn and in the *Yucky* box if they do not like the popcorn.

3. Answer the questions to compare the number of students who do and do not like the popcorn.

© *Shell Education*

Name _____

Describing Popcorn

Directions: Draw a picture. Complete each sentence.

Draw a picture of popcorn.

1. The popcorn looks 👁 _____.

2. The popcorn tastes 👄 _____.

3. The popcorn feels ✋ _____.

4. The popcorn smells 👃 _____.

5. The popcorn sounds 👂 _____.

Senses

Sense Patterns

Differentiation Strategy

 Tiered Assignments

Standards

- **Mathematics:** Students will be able to create and extend simple patterns.

- **TESOL:** Students will use English to obtain, process, construct, and provide subject matter information in spoken and written form.

Materials

- lesson resources (pages 54–57)
- scissors
- color patterns
- glue
- chart paper and markers
- salty and sweet food items (e.g., pretzels, candy)
- rough and soft objects (e.g., cotton balls, sandpaper)
- scented items (e.g., candles, spices)
- musical instruments
- art supplies

Procedures

Preparation Note: Make copies of the *Sense Pictures* activity sheet (page 54) and cut apart the cards. Make one set for each group of two to three students, plus an additional set for yourself.

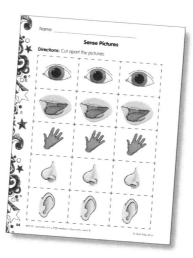

❶ Explain to the class that a pattern is a design that repeats and tells us what comes next. Display a color pattern and have students say aloud the colors in the pattern. Ask students to look at their clothes to see if they can find a pattern. Allow students with patterned clothing to share their patterns with the class.

❷ Use pictures from the *Sense Pictures* activity sheet (page 54) to create a simple AB pattern. Have extra pictures available and ask students to extend the pattern. Glue the pattern to a sheet of chart paper. After students have extended the pattern, label it with the letters A and B and encourage students to read the letters aloud. Repeat this activity, making the patterns increasingly difficult.

❸ Divide students into heterogeneous groups of no more than two to three students per group. Provide each group with a set of *Sense Pictures*. Have students take turns creating and extending patterns within their group. Encourage students to name their patterns with letters.

★ **English Language Support**—Make sure that English language learners are grouped with language-proficient students who can assist them in labeling each pattern.

Sense Patterns

④ Explain to students that they will have an opportunity to use all five of their senses to create patterns. Distribute copies of the *Making Patterns* activity sheets (pages 56–57) to students based on their readiness levels. Patterns begin simply for below-grade-level students and become more complex with on-grade-level and above-grade-level students. Distribute three copies of the *Sense Patterns Chart* activity sheet (page 55) to students for use in creating their patterns.

Activity Levels
▲
Above Grade Level
■
On Grade Level
●
Below Grade Level

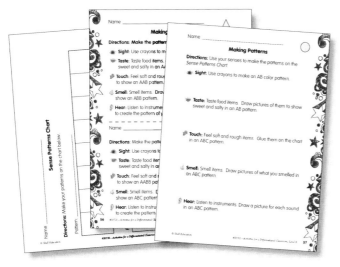

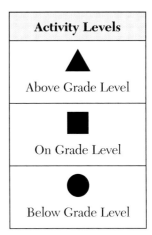

⑤ Explain the directions for each of the leveled activity sheets. Introduce the items that will be used to create patterns (e.g., pretzels, candy, cotton balls, sandpaper, scented items, musical instruments, crayons, glue) and show students how to use them. Give students time to work on their activities.

⑥ If students finish early, they may complete the Anchor Activity.

Assessment

Observe students as they create their patterns. Note which students struggle and which complete the activities with ease. Use this information to regroup students as necessary for future differentiation.

Anchor Activity

Have students create patterns using materials for two or three of the five senses. For example, they could make a pattern using a colored marker, a cotton ball, and a picture of a bell. Have students share their patterns with classmates, asking them to identify the senses used and extend and label the patterns.

Name _____

Sense Pictures

Directions: Cut apart the pictures.

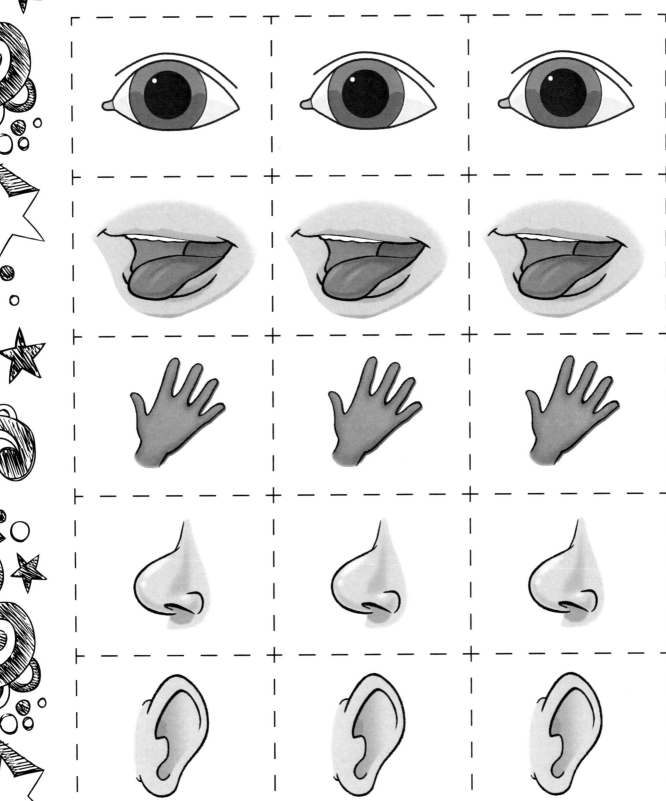

Name _____

Sense Patterns Chart

Directions: Make your patterns on the chart below.

Pattern: _____

Pattern: _____

Name _____

Making Patterns

Directions: Make the patterns on the *Sense Patterns Chart.*

Sight: Use crayons to make an ABC color pattern.

Taste: Taste food items. Draw pictures of them to show sweet and salty in an AABB pattern.

Touch: Feel soft and rough items. Glue them on the chart to show an AAB pattern.

Smell: Smell items. Draw pictures of what you smelled to show an ABB pattern.

Hear: Listen to instruments. Draw a picture for each sound to create the pattern of your choice.

- -

Name _____

Making Patterns

Directions: Make the patterns on the *Sense Patterns Chart.*

Sight: Use crayons to make an AB color pattern.

Taste: Taste food items. Draw pictures of them to show sweet and salty in an AB pattern.

Touch: Feel soft and rough items. Glue them on the chart to show an AABB pattern.

Smell: Smell items. Draw pictures of what you smelled to show an ABC pattern.

Hear: Listen to instruments. Draw a picture for each sound to create the pattern of your choice.

© Shell Education

Name _____

Making Patterns

Directions: Use your senses to make the patterns on the *Sense Patterns Chart.*

Sight: Use crayons to make an AB color pattern.

Taste: Taste food items. Draw pictures of them to show sweet and salty in an AB pattern.

Touch: Feel soft and rough items. Glue them on the chart in an ABC pattern.

Smell: Smell items. Draw pictures of what you smelled in an ABC pattern.

Hear: Listen to instruments. Draw a picture for each sound in an ABC pattern.

Making Sense of Changes

Differentiation Strategy

 Discovery Learning

Standards

- **Science:** Students will know that things can be done to materials to change some of the properties.

- **TESOL:** Students will use English to obtain, process, construct, and provide subject matter information in spoken and written form.

Materials

- lesson resources (pages 60–63)
- ice cubes
- chart paper and markers
- cups
- powdered drink mix
- water
- spoons
- watercolor paints
- paintbrushes
- food coloring

Procedures

Preparation Note: Prepare ice cubes. Set up three work stations in the classroom with the following materials:

Station 1—Copies of the *Powder Mixing* activity sheet (page 60); copies of the *Changes After Mixing* activity sheet (page 63); cups of powdered drink mix; cups of water; spoons

Station 2—Copies of the *Paint Mixing* activity sheet (page 61); copies of the *Changes After Mixing* activity sheet (page 63); watercolor paints; paintbrushes; cups of water

Station 3—Copies of the *Water Mixing* activity sheet (page 62); copies of the *Changes After Mixing* activity sheet (page 63); cups of water; food coloring; spoons

❶ Show students the cup of ice. Ask students to describe how the ice looks and feels. Pretend to be very thirsty and try to figure out a way to have the ice quench your thirst. Ask students if they know of a way to turn ice into water. Students may recommend heating it in a microwave, using body heat from their hands to warm the ice, or letting it sit out at room temperature. Tell students that you are going to place the ice on the counter. Ask them to remind you to check on it later to observe what happens to the ice. Ask students to predict what they will see when they check the ice.

Making Sense of Changes

② Create a chart with the following headings: *Heat, Freeze, Mix, Cut, Dissolve,* and *Bend.* Explain to students that there are many ways to change objects. One method of change is to add heat, as you are doing with the ice. Ask students to name other examples of changes that come from adding heat. Write their ideas in the *Heat* column of your chart. Another way to change the form of objects is by freezing them. Ask students to discuss how ice is made. Ask for other examples of freezing and write them in the *Freeze* column of the chart. Repeat discussions for *Mix* (mixing cookies or brownies), *Cut* (cutting bread or cheese), *Dissolve* (making chocolate milk with powder), and *Bend* (bending clay).

★ **English Language Support**—Discuss with English language learners what it means to heat, freeze, mix, cut, dissolve, and bend. Provide picture icons for each of these words as students complete the activities.

③ Tell students that they are about to discover how mixing can cause change. Demonstrate and explain each of the stations to the class. Allow students to select the station where they would like to work.

④ Check on the cup of ice to see if it has melted. Once the ice has turned to water, ask students to describe how it now looks and feels. Discuss what was in the cup when the lesson started and how the contents of the cup have changed over time. Remind students that the heat in the classroom caused the ice to change to water. Allow students to share what they learned about making changes to materials during their station time. Add any new ideas about change to your class chart.

⑤ If students finish early, they may complete the Anchor Activity.

Assessment

Observe students as they work in stations and ask questions to ensure that they understand the content being taught. Take notes and keep records on each student.

Anchor Activity

Have students change the forms of different materials by cutting, bending, or mixing. Give students clay, chenille craft sticks, and paper. Have them write about or draw pictures of what the materials looked like before and after. Encourage students to label their pictures.

Name _____

Powder Mixing

Directions: Use the drink mix to complete the task.

Draw a picture of what the drink mix looks 👁 like.

The drink mix smells 👃 _____ .

The drink mix feels ✋ _____ .

The drink mix tastes 👅 _____ .

1. Add water.

2. Mix.

3. Complete the *Changes After Mixing* activity sheet.

Name _____

Paint Mixing

Directions: Use the paint to complete the task.

Draw a picture of what the paint looks like.

The paint smells _____ .

The paint feels _____ .

1. Add water.

2. Mix.

3. Complete the *Changes After Mixing* activity sheet.

Name _____

Water Mixing

Directions: Use the water to complete the task.

Draw a picture of what the water looks 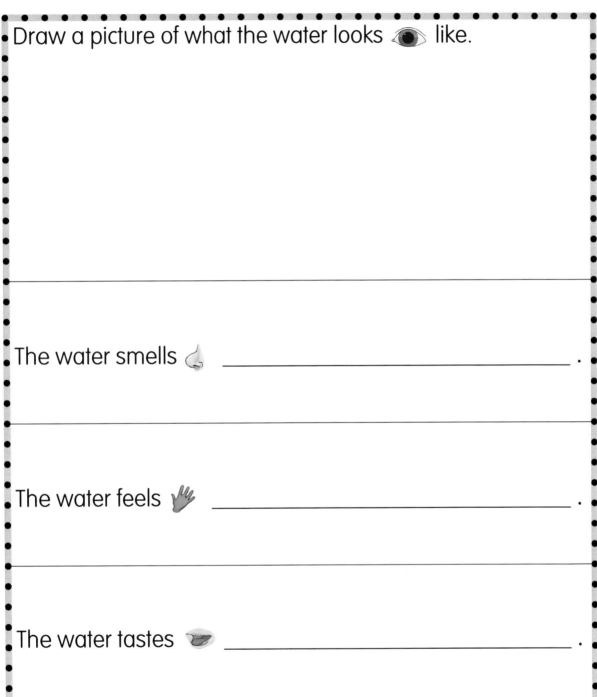 like.

The water smells _____ .

The water feels _____ .

The water tastes _____ .

1. Add food coloring.

2. Mix.

3. Complete the *Changes After Mixing* activity sheet.

Name _____

Changes After Mixing

Directions: Answer the questions below.

What material did you start with? _____

What did you mix with the water? _____	Draw a picture of what the new mixture looks 👁 like.

It smells 👃 _____.
It feels ✋ _____.
Is this something you can taste? If not, skip this box. It tastes 👄 _____.

Circle the best answer below:

Does it look 👁 the same?	Yes	No
Does it smell 👃 the same?	Yes	No
Does it feel ✋ the same?	Yes	No
If you can taste 👄 the new mixture, does it taste the same?	Yes	No

Sensing My World

Differentiation Strategy

 Multiple Intelligences

Standards

- **Social Studies:** Students will know that people use their senses to find out about their surroundings.

- **TESOL:** Students will use English to obtain, process, construct, and provide subject matter information in spoken and written form.

Materials

- lesson resources (pages 66–69)
- *Sense Pictures* (page 54)
- crayons or markers
- watercolor paints
- paint brushes
- scissors
- stapler

Procedures

Preparation Note: Set up four Multiple Intelligences stations in the classroom with the appropriate portion of the *Sensing My World Stations* activity sheets (pages 66-67) and the following materials:

Naturalist Station—Drawing paper; crayons or markers; pencils

Interpersonal Station—Copies of the *Sense Pictures* activity sheet (page 54); copies of the *Places in My Community* activity sheet (page 68); scissors

Bodily/Kinesthetic Station—Drawing paper; black crayons; watercolor paints; paintbrushes

Verbal/Linguistic and **Visual/Spatial Station**—Copies of the *Sensing My Community Book* activity sheet (page 69); crayons or markers; pencils; scissors; stapler

1 Ask students to name the five senses. Have them tell how

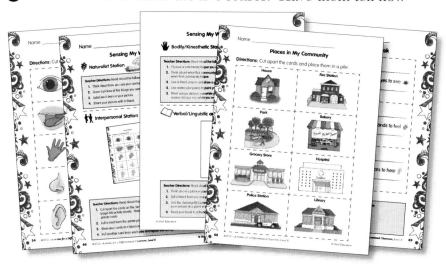

they use each of their senses at school every day. Explain that during some parts of the day, they use one sense more than others. For example, while being read a story, they are mostly using their senses of listening and looking, but while eating, they are mostly using their senses of taste and smell.

Sensing My World

❷ If possible, take a walk around the school. Discuss what senses are being used. Stop at different areas such as the lunchroom, gym, music room, computer lab, and office (if you are not able to take a walk, ask students to think about each area). Ask students to name different things they might see, taste, feel, smell, and hear in each area. Have them think about whether one sense is being used more than others at each of these places.

★ **English Language Support**—Keep English language learners involved in identifying which of the five senses would be used most by touching their eyes (sight), nose (smell), ears (hearing), mouth (taste), and fingertips (touch).

❸ When you return to the classroom, divide the students into heterogeneous groups. Assign each group a different place in the school and have them draw or write about how their senses are used in that area. After they finish, gather the class together and allow each group to share how they use their senses at school.

❹ Distribute copies of the *Sensing My World Stations* activity sheets (pages 66–67) to students. Tell students that they will have an opportunity to learn about using their senses in the community while completing their center activities. Provide students with additional activity sheets and any materials needed to help them complete the activities.

❺ Demonstrate and explain the activities to students.

❻ If students finish early, they may complete the Anchor Activity.

Assessment

Note which activity students choose and how successful they are at completing the activity. Conference with students to determine why they chose the activities they did. Keep records of their strengths within the multiple intelligences to use in selecting future differentiation tasks for students.

Anchor Activity

Have students choose a sense. Tell them to think of a place in the community where that sense is used the most. Ask students to draw a picture of the place they selected in the middle of a large sheet of paper. Around the edges of their paper, have students draw pictures of how their sense is used in that particular place. Encourage students to label or write sentences about their pictures.

Name _____

Sensing My World Stations

 ## Naturalist Station

Teacher Directions: Read aloud the following directions to students:

1. Think about how you use your senses at the park.

2. Draw a picture of the things you see, taste, feel, smell, and hear at the park.

3. Label each item in your picture.

4. Share your picture with a friend.

Name _____

 ## Interpersonal Station

Teacher Directions: Read aloud the following directions to students:

1. Cut apart the cards on the *Sense Pictures* (page 54) and *Places in My Community* (page 68) activity sheets. Make two piles: one pile of *sense* cards and one pile of *places* cards.

2. Pull a card from the *sense* pile and then pull a card from the *places* pile.

3. Show your cards to a friend and tell him or her how you use your sense in that place.

4. Pull another card from each pile and repeat the activity.

Name _____

Sensing My World Stations *(cont.)*

 Bodily/Kinesthetic Station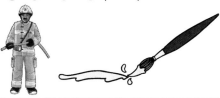

Teacher Directions: Read aloud the following directions to students:

1. Choose a community helper you would like to be when you grow up.

2. Think about what that community helper does. Act out what you would do if you were that community helper.

3. Use a black crayon and draw a picture of your community helper working.

4. Use watercolor paints to paint your picture.

5. What senses did you use while you were acting like the community helper? What senses did you use while you were painting? Tell a friend.

- -

Name _____

 Verbal/Linguistic and **Visual/Spatial Station**

My School
School

Teacher Directions: Read aloud the following directions to students:

1. Think about a place in your community you like to visit.

2. Tell a friend how you use your senses when you visit this place.

3. Use the *Sensing My Community Book* (page 69) pages to write a book about using your senses at a place in your community.

4. Read your book to a friend.

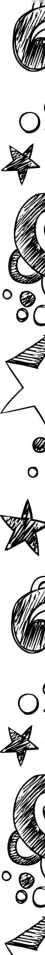

Name _____

Places in My Community

Directions: Cut apart the cards and place them in a pile.

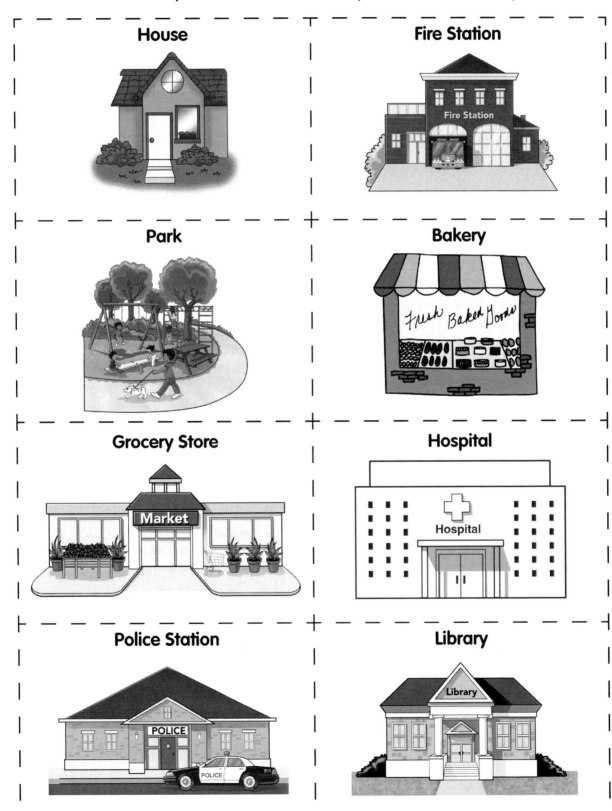

House

Fire Station

Park

Bakery

Grocery Store

Hospital

Police Station

Library

Name _____

Sensing My Community Book

A Visit to _____

By _____

At the _____

I use my eyes to see

_____ .

At the _____

I use my mouth to taste

_____ .

At the _____

I use my hands to feel

_____ .

At the _____

I use my nose to smell

_____ .

At the _____

I use my ears to hear

_____ .

Teacher Directions: Read aloud the following directions to students:

1. Choose a place in your community.
2. Think about how you use your senses at that place.
3. Draw pictures and write words on the pages of this book.
4. Cut the pages apart and staple them into a book.

People, Places, and Things in My Community

Differentiation Strategy

 Leveled Learning Centers

Standards

- **Language Arts:** Students will use nouns in written compositions.

- **TESOL:** Students will use English to obtain, process, construct, and provide subject matter information in spoken and written form.

Materials

- lesson resources (pages 72–75)

- pictures of community helpers, places they work, and things they use

- chart paper and markers

- crayons

- scissors

- paper lunch bags

- art supplies

Procedures

Preparation Note: Set up three centers in the classroom with the following materials:

Center 1—Copies of *Mixed-Up Community* (page 72); lined paper; pencils; scissors

Center 2—Copies of *Community Helpers* (page 73); lined paper; pencils

Center 3—Copies of *People and Places* (page 74); paper lunch bags; scissors; art supplies

❶ Draw three columns on a large sheet of chart paper. Label the columns *People*, *Places*, and *Things*. Tell students that one part of a sentence is a *noun*. Write the word *noun* at the top of your chart. Explain that a noun can be a person, a place, or a thing. Tell students that you are a teacher and a teacher is a person. Write *teacher* in the *People* column on the chart. Ask students where you work. Write *school* in the *Places* column. Finally, ask students to name some of the items that you use. Write these items in the *Things* column. Show students pictures of community helpers. Help students sort pictures into the correct category and attach them to the chart.

★ **English Language Support**—Have students act out the jobs of community helpers. Bring real examples of things that community helpers use into the classroom. Allow English language learners to use pictures, actions, and real-life facts when completing the activities.

❷ At the top of a sheet of chart paper, write the sentence frame *A _____ is a community helper. This helper _____.* Ask students to name a community helper and have them help you write the name of that helper in the first blank. Have students tell what that helper does. Write what the helper does in the second blank. Read the sentences together as a class. For example, if talking about a doctor, you may write *This helper takes care of me when I'm sick.* See if students can identify the word *helper* as the noun in the sentence. Practice writing sentences using other community helpers and other sentence frames. For example, *A _____ (community helper) works at a _____ (place)*, and *A _____ (community helper) uses _____ (thing) to work.*

People, Places, and Things in My Community

3 Divide the class into heterogeneous groups. Tell students to select a person, a place where he or she works, and an item that he or she uses from the list. Have students draw a picture of each noun they selected. As they work on their drawings, have students form a sentence using their nouns. Encourage students to write the sentence below their drawings if they are able. Once students have completed their drawings, allow them to share with the class.

4 Tell students that they will have more practice writing nouns about community helpers in their learning centers. Explain each activity sheet and answer any questions students have.

5 Assign students a shape based on their readiness levels. Tell students that they will complete the activity at each center that matches the shape assigned to them.

6 Assign students to one of the three learning centers. After giving students enough time to finish their work, have the groups rotate. Repeat this until all students have visited each of the three centers.

7 If students finish early, they may complete the Anchor Activity.

Activity Levels
▲
Above Grade Level
■
On Grade Level
●
Below Grade Level

Assessment

Use the *My Community Rubric* (page 75) to assess students at different levels. Below-grade-level and on-grade-level students who score in the *Working at Advanced Level* column may need to be moved to a higher level for future differentiated lessons in this content area, while above-grade-level students who scored in the *Needs Additional Support* column may need to be moved to the on-grade-level group.

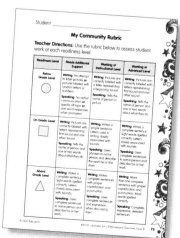

Anchor Activity

Have students create their own *People, Places,* and *Things* chart about your school. Ask students to make a chart similar to the one you made for the class activity. Then, have them draw pictures of people who work at the school, places where they work, and things that they use. Encourage students to label their pictures. Students could write or tell a story about school workers, if time allows.

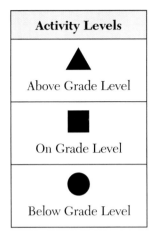

Name _____

Mixed-Up Community

△ Use the words to make up a story.

◯ Say the names of the pictures.

▢ Make sentences using the words.

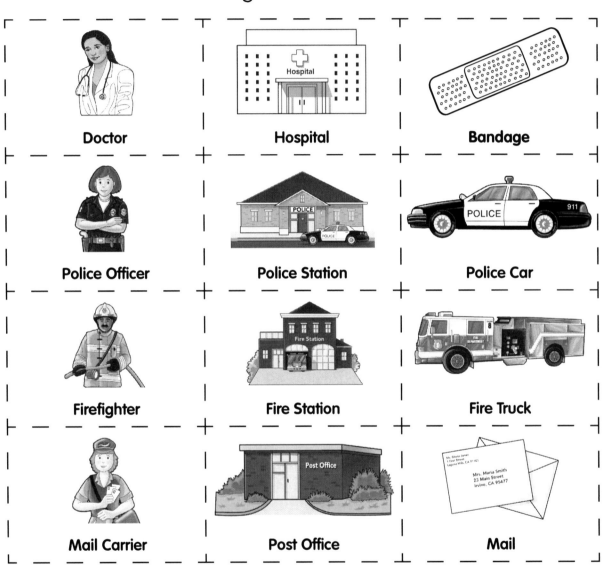

Doctor	**Hospital**	**Bandage**
Police Officer	**Police Station**	**Police Car**
Firefighter	**Fire Station**	**Fire Truck**
Mail Carrier	**Post Office**	**Mail**

Teacher Directions: Read aloud the following directions to students:

1. Cut the boxes apart.

2. Mix up the cards.

3. Sort the cards into three stacks: *People, Places,* and *Things.*

4. Follow the directions by your shape.

Name _____

Community Helpers

◯ Label your pictures as *person*, *place*, or *thing*.

△ Write a sentence about each picture. Circle the nouns in your sentences.

▢ Write one sentence telling about your pictures. Circle one noun in your sentence.

Community Helper	Where the Helper Works	Item the Helper Uses

_____

_____

_____

Teacher Directions: Read aloud the following directions to students:

1. Draw a picture of a community helper, the place where the community helper works, and an item the community helper uses.

2. Remember that a *noun* is a person, place, or thing.

3. Follow the directions by your shape.

Name _____

People and Places

Directions: Think of a person in your community. Follow the directions by your shape:

Make a puppet. Tell about its job.

Make two puppets. Have them talk.

Make two puppets. Make tools for each puppet to use. Have them talk.

Student _____

My Community Rubric

Teacher Directions: Use the rubric below to assess student work at each readiness level.

Readiness Level	Needs Additional Support	Working at Instructional Level	Working at Advanced Level
Below Grade Level	**Writing:** No attempt to label pictures **or** pictures labeled with random letters or numbers. **Speaking:** No verbal communication **or** speaks off topic **or** one-word responses when prompted.	**Writing:** Pictures are correctly labeled with a letter representing a beginning sound. **Speaking:** Tells the name of person in picture.	**Writing:** Pictures are correctly labeled with letters representing first sound and one other sound. **Speaking:** Tells the name of person and one or two words about what they do.
On Grade Level	**Writing:** Pictures are correctly labeled with letters representing first sound and one other sound. **Speaking:** Tells the name of person and one or two words about what they do.	**Writing:** Writes a simple sentence. Letters used in writing closely associated with sounds. **Speaking:** Uses phrases to name person and describe the work he or she does.	**Writing:** Writes a complete sentence. Sight words spelled correctly. Letters closely associated with sounds. **Speaking:** Uses complete sentences to name person and describe his or her work.
Above Grade Level	**Writing:** Writes a complete sentence. Sight words spelled correctly. Letters closely associated with sounds. **Speaking:** Uses complete sentences to name person and describe his or her work.	**Writing:** Writes complete sentences with proper capitalization and punctuation. **Speaking:** Uses complete sentences and expression when discussing topic.	**Writing:** More than one complete sentence with proper capitalization and punctuation. Most words spelled correctly. **Speaking:** Complete, expressive, detailed sentences.

Shaping Up My Community

Differentiation Strategy

Bloom's Taxonomy

Standards

- **Mathematics:** Students will know that geometric shapes are useful for representing and describing real-world situations.

- **TESOL:** Students will use English to obtain, process, construct, and provide subject matter information in spoken and written form.

Materials

- lesson resources (pages 78–81)
- scissors
- index cards
- large construction paper
- art supplies
- glue
- chart paper and markers
- precut shapes
- books and pictures of police cars, fire trucks, community helpers *(See page 167.)*
- pictures of table settings or dishes

Procedures

Preparation Note: Cut apart the activity cards on the *Community Helpers and Shapes* activity sheet (page 78). Prepare the following materials for each of the Bloom's Taxonomy activities in this lesson:

Remembering—Copies of the *Shape Hunt* activity sheet (page 81)

Understanding—Books or pictures of community helpers; paper; crayons; two sets of index cards, one with pictures of shapes (square, circle, triangle, oval, rhombus, rectangle), and the other with names of the same shapes

Applying—Precut shapes (six shapes listed above); paper; glue

Analyzing—Copies of *Riding Along With Shapes* (page 80); pictures of police cars and fire trucks; precut shapes (six shapes listed above); paper; glue

Creating—Copies of *Imagine This* (page 79); books or pictures of community helpers

Evaluating—Pictures of table settings or dishes; five blank sheets of paper stapled together to make a *Restaurant Book*; crayons

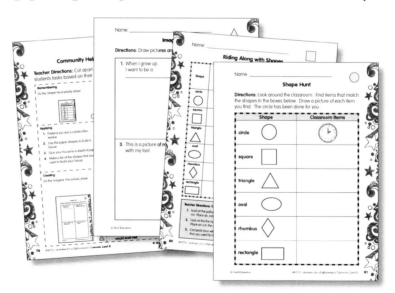

❶ Show students the shape cards. Ask students to identify each shape and match the shape with its name.

★ **English Language Support**—Provide English language learners with labeled cards containing pictures of geometric shapes and the names of the shapes to use as a reference throughout the activity.

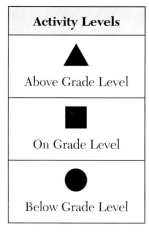

Shaping Up My Community

2 Divide the class into heterogeneous groups. Give each group a shape card and a sheet of construction paper. Have groups look in the classroom to find objects that match their shape. Ask students to draw each object they find on their paper and label their drawings. Gather students together and allow groups to share their drawings.

3 As a group, explain to students that the various shaped objects they found in the classroom are tools teachers and students use for doing their jobs. Other community workers have tools that they use in their work. Ask students to brainstorm community helpers. Record a list of these helpers on a sheet of chart paper. Next, ask students to name tools that each community helper uses. List or draw these tools on your chart.

4 Distribute the cut-apart *Community Helpers and Shapes* activity cards (page 78) to students based on their readiness levels. Below-grade-level students will also receive *Shape Hunt* (page 81). On-grade-level students will receive *Riding Along with Shapes* (page 80). Above-grade-level students will receive *Imagine This* (page 79). Demonstrate how to complete each activity.

5 Monitor students as they work on assignments and provide assistance as needed.

6 If students finish early, they may complete the Anchor Activity.

Assessment

Observe students as they work at different levels of Bloom's Taxonomy. Keep anecdotal records about students' performance. Note those students who may be ready for a higher-level challenge during future differentiated lessons.

Activity Levels
▲
Above Grade Level
■
On Grade Level
●
Below Grade Level

Anchor Activity

Have students select a community helper and think about where that helper works. Provide shape cutouts. Ask students to create a picture of where the community helper works. They can either trace or glue shapes to their paper to make the picture. Ask students to use at least four of the shapes in their pictures. When students have completed their pictures, have them give their paper to a friend and ask the friend to identify the shapes in the picture.

Community Helpers and Shapes

Teacher Directions: Cut apart the cards below. Assign students tasks based on their readiness levels.

Remembering

Do the *Shape Hunt* activity sheet.

Understanding

1. Draw a picture of a community helper.
2. Think of the tools that this helper uses and draw them on your paper.
3. Write the shape name next to your tool.

Applying

1. Pretend you are a construction worker.
2. Use the paper shapes to build a house.
3. Glue your house to a sheet of paper.
4. Make a list of the shapes that you used to build your house.

Analyzing

1. Use the paper shapes to make a police car and fire truck.
2. Glue them to a sheet of paper.
3. Do the *Riding Along with Shapes* activity sheet.

Creating

Do the *Imagine This* activity sheet.

Evaluating

1. Think about a restaurant and the shapes you see there.
2. On each page of the restaurant book, draw pictures of a table, a plate, a cup, a napkin, and a menu. Write the shape name of each object you drew.
3. Now think of new shapes for each object. For example, you might have a square plate rather than a round one. Recommend a new shape for each object.
4. Draw a picture of the recommended object on the page with the first object you drew. Be ready to explain why the new shape for the object would work well.

Name _____

Imagine This

Directions: Draw pictures and write words to fill in the boxes.

1. When I grow up
I want to be a

_____ .

2. I made this tool.
It helps me do my job.

3. This is a picture of me
with my tool.

4. This is the shape of
my tool.

Name _____

Riding Along with Shapes

Shape	Police Car	Fire Truck	Police Car and Fire Truck
circle			
square			
triangle			
oval			
rhombus			
rectangle			

Teacher Directions: Read aloud the following directions to students:

1. Look at the police car you made. Find each shape you used to make your police car. Place an *x* in the first column by each shape you used for the police car.

2. Look at the fire truck you made. Find each shape you used to make your fire truck. Place an *x* in the second column by each shape you used for the fire truck.

3. Compare your vehicles. In the third column, place a happy face by each shape that you used for both vehicles.

Name _____

Shape Hunt

Directions: Look around the classroom. Find items that match the shapes in the boxes below. Draw a picture of each item you find. The circle has been done for you.

Shape	Classroom Items
circle	
square	
triangle	
oval	
rhombus	
rectangle	

Tools in the Community

Differentiation Strategy

 Tiered Assignments

Standards

- **Science:** Students will know that tools can be used to gather information and extend the senses.

- **TESOL:** Students will use English to obtain, process, construct, and provide subject matter information in spoken and written form.

Materials

- lesson resources (pages 84–87)

- pictures of community helpers using thermometers, magnifying glasses, rulers, and yardsticks

- thermometers

- magnifying glasses

- rulers and yardsticks

- art supplies

Procedures

❶ Tell students that they are going to learn about tools used by community helpers. These tools assist community helpers in collecting information and learning as they work.

❷ Display and ask students to identify thermometers, magnifying glasses, rulers, and yardsticks. Talk about each tool and how it is used. You may wish to pass the tools around and allow time for students to experiment with the various tools. Gather materials and ask students to share what they know about each tool.

★ **English Language Support**—Allow students to practice using tools (thermometers, magnifying glasses, rulers, and yardsticks). Provide pictures of community helpers using these tools for extra support.

❸ Divide the class into three heterogeneous groups. Give each group one tool, a large sheet of paper, and crayons or markers. Allow students to try using the tools in their groups. Ask them to draw pictures of community helpers who would use the tool and how they would use it. Encourage students to label their pictures. When students have completed their group work, gather the class together. Have each group share their tool and ways in which it is used by community helpers.

❹ Divide students into three homogeneous groups based on readiness levels and have them sit at tables or desks grouped together. Tell students that they will have an opportunity to learn more about how community helpers use these tools.

Tools in the Community

5 Distribute copies of the *Tools Community Helpers Use* activity sheets (pages 84–86) to each group based on their readiness levels.

Activity Levels
▲
Above Grade Level
■
On Grade Level
●
Below Grade Level

6 Walk around to each group and explain the directions, beginning with the below-grade-level students. Allow students to work together. Circulate around the classroom to assist each group, but stay near the below-grade-level students to answer any questions and to make sure they stay on task.

7 If students finish early, they may complete the Anchor Activity.

Assessment

Evaluate the assignments that students complete. If below-grade-level and on-grade-level students successfully completed their assignments, they may need to be moved to a higher group for future differentiated lessons in this content area. Above-grade-level and on-grade-level students who struggled with their work may need to be assigned to a lower group in the future.

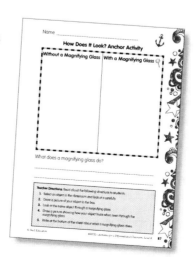

Anchor Activity ⚓

Have students practice making observations with a magnifying glass. Provide copies of the *How Does It Look? Anchor Activity* (page 87), magnifying glasses, and a container of objects for students to observe, such as cotton balls, coins, or shells.

Name _____

Tools Community Helpers Use

Tools	Community Helper 1	How Tool Is Used
Thermometer 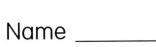		
Magnifying Glass		
Ruler or Yardstick		

Teacher Directions: Read aloud the following directions to students:

1. Draw a picture of a community helper who might use each tool.

2. Explain how the tool helps the community helper.

Name _____

Tools Community Helpers Use

Tools	Community Helper 1	Community Helper 2
Thermometer		
Magnifying Glass		
Ruler or Yardstick		

Teacher Directions: Read the directions below aloud to students.

1. Draw a picture of two community helpers who might use each tool.

2. Show the helpers using the tool in your drawing.

3. Label your drawings.

Name _____

Tools Community Helpers Use

Tools	Community Helper
Thermometer	
Magnifying Glass	
Ruler or Yardstick	

Teacher Directions: Read aloud the following directions to students:

1. Draw a picture of a community helper who might use each tool.

Name _____

How Does It Look? Anchor Activity

Without a Magnifying Glass	With a Magnifying Glass 🔍

What does a magnifying glass do?

_____

_____

Teacher Directions: Read aloud the following directions to students:

1. Select an object in the classroom and look at it carefully.

2. Draw a picture of your object in the box.

3. Look at the same object through a magnifying glass.

4. Draw a picture showing how your object looks when seen through the magnifying glass.

5. Write at the bottom of the sheet about what a magnifying glass does.

Community Goods and Services

Differentiation Strategy

Choices Board

Standards

- **Social Studies:** Students will understand that goods are objects that can satisfy people's wants and services are activities that can satisfy people's wants.

- **TESOL:** Students will use English to obtain, process, construct, and provide subject matter information in spoken and written form.

Materials

- lesson resources (pages 90–93)
- shopping bag
- school supplies
- chart paper and markers
- pictures of goods and services, picture books of community helpers *(See page 167.)*
- clay
- art supplies

Procedures

1 Show students a shopping bag filled with items you use at school. Pull items out of the bag and ask students to identify each object. Tell students that these are things you wanted for school. Explain that objects or things that you buy are called *goods*. Write the word *goods* at the top of a sheet of chart paper. List the goods that were in your bag.

★ **English Language Support**—Provide English language learners with picture examples of different goods and services.

2 Ask students where they go when they are not feeling well. Have them explain what a doctor does when they are sick. Tell students that a doctor helps make you feel better. When the doctor helps you feel better, he or she is providing a service. Services are activities done by people in the community. Write the word *services* on the top of a sheet of chart paper. Draw a picture of a doctor helping a person feel better on the chart. Ask students to think of other services provided by community helpers and discuss these as a class.

3 Divide the class into two groups. Give one group the *goods* chart and the other group the *services* chart. Have each group add to the list. They can draw pictures and label them if they are able. Meet again as a whole group to discuss the goods and services that students have listed. Ask students to name the community helper who provides each good and service.

4 Tell students that they will learn more about goods and services as they complete activities on the class choices board. Assign students a shape based on their readiness levels. Explain the *Choosing Goods and Services Choices Board* (page 90) activities to students. Tell students that they will complete at least two activities that match the shape assigned to them.

Community Goods and Services

❺ Explain and demonstrate each of the activity choices. For three activities on the choices board, an additional activity sheet is required. These include the *Goods and Services Graph* activity sheet (page 91), the *Goods and Services T-Chart* activity sheet (page 92), and the *Community Helper Match* activity sheet (page 93). Provide students with any needed materials to help them complete the activities.

Activity Levels
▲
Above Grade Level
■
On Grade Level
●
Below Grade Level

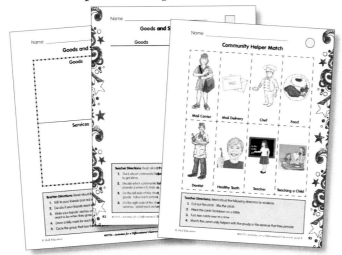

❻ If students finish early, they may complete the Anchor Actvity.

Assessment

Evaluate the activities students complete from the choices board to ensure that lesson objectives have been met. Keep records of students' progress toward set goals.

Anchor Activity

Have students create a chart displaying different goods and services. Ask students to think about the goods and services they drew and then decide which are things they need and which are things they want. Have students circle the goods or services they need with a green crayon. Have them circle the goods and services they want with a yellow crayon.

Choosing Goods and Services Choices Board

Teacher Directions: Explain the Choices Board activity options below to students.

Choose a community helper who provides a service. Think about what that helper does. Pretend to be that community helper. Act out the service that the community helper provides. See if a friend can name your community helper. You will need pictures of community helpers. ○	Make a chart of community helpers who provide goods and community helpers who provide services. You will need the *Goods and Services T-Chart*. □	Look at or read a book about a community helper. Draw a picture of a community helper from the book. Does the community helper provide a good or a service? Write a sentence about what the community helper does. You will need books about community helpers. △
Ask your friends what they want to be when they grow up. Decide if your friend will provide a good or a service. Record their information on the chart. You will need the *Goods and Services Graph*. △	Pretend you are a baker. Use clay to make goods you might sell at your bakery. ○	Draw a picture of a community helper that you might be when you grow up. Be sure to draw the goods or service that you will provide. □
Choose a community helper who provides goods. Draw a picture of that community helper and the goods he or she gives us. □	Choose a community helper whom you would like to be when you grow up. Make a poster showing the community helper and the goods or services that you will provide. △	Play a matching game. Match the community helpers with the goods or services they provide. Sort the cards into piles of goods and services. You will need the *Community Helper Match*. ○

Name _____

Goods and Services Graph

Goods	Tally Marks

Services	Tally Marks

Teacher Directions: Read aloud the following directions to students:

1. Talk to your friends and ask what they want to be when they grow up.

2. Decide if your friends want to provide a good or a service.

3. Write your friends' names on the chart under *Goods* or *Services* and what they want to be when they grow up. You may draw a picture, too.

4. Draw a tally mark for each friend's name.

5. Circle the group that has the most people.

Name _____

Goods and Services T-Chart

Goods	Services

Teacher Directions: Read aloud the following directions to students:

1. Think about community helpers. You may want to look at our class chart or books to get ideas.

2. Decide which community helpers provide goods for us to use, and which helpers provide a service to help us.

3. On the left side of this chart, draw pictures of community helpers who provide goods. Label each picture.

4. On the right side of the chart, draw pictures of community helpers who provide services. Label each picture.

Name _____

Community Helper Match

| Mail Carrier | Mail Delivery | Chef | Food |
| Dentist | Healthy Teeth | Teacher | Teaching a Child |

Teacher Directions: Read aloud the following directions to students:

1. Cut out the cards. Mix the cards.
2. Place the cards facedown on a table.
3. Turn two cards over at a time.
4. Match the community helpers with the goods or the services that they provide.

Building Stories

Differentiation Strategy

Multiple Intelligences

Standards

- **Language Arts:** Students will know the setting, main characters, main events, sequence, and problems in stories.

- **TESOL:** Students will use English to obtain, process, construct, and provide subject matter information in spoken and written form.

Materials

- lesson resources (pages 96–99)
- chart paper and markers
- fairy tale story or book
- magnetic letters or letter flash cards
- sentence strips
- 6" x 3" red construction paper rectangles
- glue
- craft sticks
- art supplies

Procedures

Preparation Note: Set up four Multiple Intelligences stations in the classroom with the following materials:

Logical/Mathematical—Copies of the *Building a Story* activity sheet (page 97); pencils; crayons

Interpersonal—Copies of the *Building Characters* activity sheet (page 98); 12" x 18" construction paper; scissors; glue; pencils; crayons

Bodily/Kinesthetic—Copies of the *Building a Puppet Show* activity sheet (page 96); construction paper scraps; scissors; glue; crayons; craft sticks

Visual/Spatial—Copies of the *Building the Setting* activity sheet (page 99); paint (assorted colors); paint brushes; 12" x 18" white paper; pencils

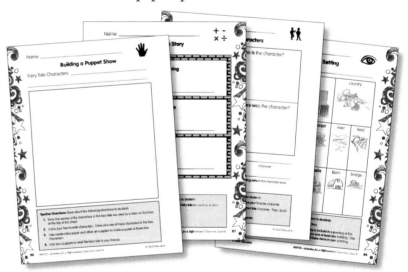

Before teaching the lesson, divide a large piece of chart paper into three sections. Label one section *Characters*, the next section *Setting*, and the last section *Events*. Write on a sentence strip the sentence *We are going to build stories today*. Once the sentence has been written, cut apart the sentence strip between each word.

❶ Tell students that they are going to be builders. Explain that just as construction workers use tools and materials to build a house, writers use words to build stories. Students will have the opportunity to build stories using letters and words. Show students some magnetic letters and allow them to help you use those letters to build words.

② Display the words from the sentence that you cut apart (see Preparation Note) in an incorrect order. Help students understand that words have to come in a certain order to make sense and be a meaningful part of the story. Allow students to work together to place the words in the correct order. Read the sentence aloud as a class.

③ Show students the *Characters*, *Setting*, and *Events* chart and explain that these are components writers use to build a story. Refer to a fairy tale that you have previously read in class or read one aloud. Ask students to name the characters and setting in this fairy tale. Write each character's name and the setting on a piece of red construction paper cut into a rectangle to look like a brick and attach it to the chart. Explain that you are using this "brick" to "build" the story. Finally, ask the students to recall the events that happened in the story. Explain the importance of putting events in proper sequence for the story to make sense. Write down each event on a brick to add to your chart's *Events* column.

★ **English Language Support**—Provide English language learners with cards depicting characters and setting. Discuss the people and places on the cards. Allow students to orally tell about the sequence of events in the fairy tale.

④ Explain to students that they will have the opportunity to build stories while completing their activities. Explain each station activity to the class. Assign students to a station to begin working. Walk around to each station to assist students.

⑤ Provide students time to work at the different stations. When students finish their work, divide them into small groups and allow them to share what they have done.

⑥ If students finish early, they may complete the Anchor Activity.

Assessment

Hold one-on-one conferences with students. As students share their work with you, assess their understanding of building stories. Keep a record of each student's proficiency level on this standard.

Anchor Activity

Have students build a fairy tale. Give students sheets of paper stapled in book form. Have them include characters and establish a setting. Tell students that the story must be in the correct sequence to make sense. Encourage students to write words to go along with their story. Provide an opportunity for students to share their completed stories with the class.

Name _____

Building a Puppet Show

Fairy Tale Characters _____

_____

┌───┐
│   │
│   │
│   │
│   │
│   │
│   │
│   │
│   │
│   │
│   │
│   │
└───┘

Teacher Directions: Read aloud the following directions to students:

1. Write the names of the characters in the fairy tale we read as a class on the lines at the top of this sheet.

2. Circle your two favorite characters. Draw pictures of these characters in the box.

3. Use construction paper and other art supplies to make puppets of those two characters.

4. Use your puppets to retell the fairy tale to your friends.

Name _____

+ -
× ÷

Building a Story

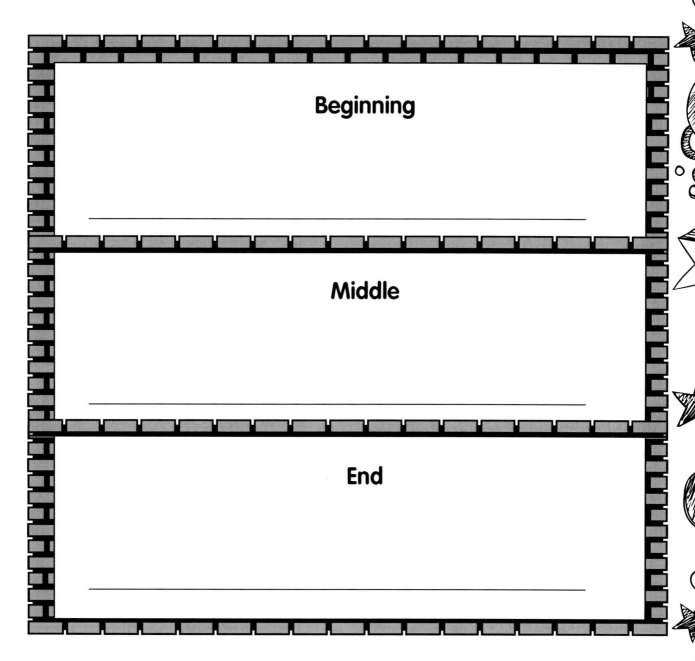

Beginning

_____

Middle

_____

End

_____

Teacher Directions: Read aloud the following directions to students:

1. Think about the beginning, middle, and end of the fairy tale we read as a class.
2. Draw a picture for each part in each section.
3. Write a sentence for each picture.
4. Tell a friend about the parts of the fairy tale.

Name _____

Building Characters

Tell about the character.	Who is the character?
What did the character do?	**Where was the character?**

_____   _____
Describe   Character

_____   _____
Action (what the character did)   Setting (where the character was)

Teacher Directions: Read aloud the following directions to students:

1. Think about the fairy tale we read as a class. Choose your favorite character.

2. Fill in the boxes at the top of this sheet to help tell about this character. Then, build a sentence about your character on the lines below.

3. On a sheet of paper, draw a picture of the character.

4. Tell a friend about your favorite character.

Name _____

Building the Setting

Title of the fairy tale: _____

Land	mountain	forest
	river	field
Buildings	houses castle	barn bridge

Teacher Directions: Read aloud the following directions to students:

1. Design a setting for the fairy tale we read as a class.

2. Circle the pictures of the items that you would like to include in a painting of this fairy tale setting. Choose at least one land feature and at least one building. Use these items in your painting. Try to label each of these items in your painting.

Building Towers

Differentiation Strategy

Discovery Learning

Standards

- **Mathematics:** Students will understand basic estimation strategies and terms.

- **TESOL:** Students will use English to obtain, process, construct, and provide subject matter information in spoken and written form.

Materials

- lesson resources (pages 102–105)

- snap cubes

- interlocking bricks, large craft sticks, blocks

- number cards

- stickers

- sticky notes

- *Rapunzel* by the Brothers Grimm (*See page 167.*)

- yarn

Procedures

Preparation Note: Before class begins, set up three different workstations in the room. Use the list below to plan for supplies at each workstation.

Station 1: A Block Tower for Rapunzel—Copies of *A Block Tower for Rapunzel* (page 103); a piece of yarn representing Rapunzel's hair (5"–9" long, depending on the size blocks you use); snap cubes

Station 2: A Stick Tower for Rapunzel—Copies of *A Stick Tower for Rapunzel* (page 104); a piece of yarn representing Rapunzel's hair (3"–5" long, depending on the size sticks you use); large craft sticks

Station 3: A Brick Tower for Rapunzel—Copies of *A Brick Tower for Rapunzel* (page 105); a piece of yarn representing Rapunzel's hair (6"–9" long, depending on the size bricks you use); interlocking bricks (such as Legos®)

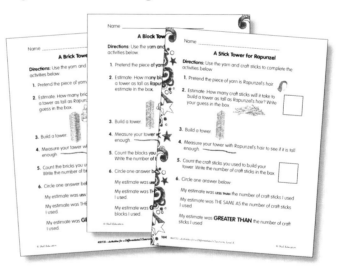

Prior to teaching the lesson, build a tower of interlocking cubes. Set aside.

★ **English Language Support**—Provide English language learners with a set of number cards (1–5) and stickers to practice one-to-one correspondence. Have students read the number on each card and attach that number of stickers to their card. Ask students to identify which cards have a greater number of stickers and which cards have a smaller number of stickers.

Building Towers

1 Begin the class lesson by showing students the tower of cubes you built and one cube next to it. Explain that students can use the size of one cube to estimate how many cubes you used to build your tower. Give each child a sticky note. Ask them all to write their name and an estimate of the number of cubes used on the sticky note. Have students take turns putting their sticky notes on the board.

2 Ask students to help you count the number of cubes used to build your tower. Count each cube aloud with students. Write the actual number of cubes used on the board.

3 Look at the numbers that the students estimated. Have students identify each number and determine if it is greater than or less than the actual number of cubes used. Place the numbers that are less than the actual number to the left of the number you wrote. Place the numbers that are greater to the right of the actual number. You may wish to use students' numbers to create a number line on your board.

4 Read the fairy tale *Rapunzel* to the class. As you read the story, use the picture cards provided in the *Fairy Tale People, Places, and Things* activity sheet (page 102) to help students understand the fairy tale vocabulary. After reading, discuss the characters, setting, and plot of the story. Help students understand that the witch and the prince were able to climb up Rapunzel's hair to her window because her hair reached from the window to the ground.

5 Tell students that they will perform experiments at stations to build towers for Rapunzel. Demonstrate and explain each of the stations to students. Divide the class into three groups and assign one station to each group.

6 Monitor the groups and provide assistance as necessary. When all students have completed their towers, have each group share its work. Conclude by having students summarize what they learned during the activity.

7 If students finish early, they may complete the Anchor Activity.

Assessment

Observe students as they work and ask questions to determine whether the lesson objectives have been met.

Anchor Activity

Have students work in small groups to build a tower for Rapunzel. Provide other materials such as dominoes, index or playing cards, or items from their desks. First, have students estimate the number of objects they will use to build their towers. Then, allow them to build towers. When they have completed their towers, have students count the actual number of items they used to create their towers.

Name _____

Fairy Tale People, Places, and Things

castle

bridge

tower

forest

mountains

pond

river

fairy

prince

princess

Teacher Directions: Cut apart and use these picture cards throughout the lessons in this unit to help students identify fairy tale elements.

Name _____

A Block Tower for Rapunzel

Directions: Use the yarn and blocks to complete the activities below.

1. Pretend the piece of yarn is Rapunzel's hair.

2. Estimate: How many blocks will it take to build a tower as tall as Rapunzel's hair? Write your estimate in the box.

3. Build a tower.

4. Measure your tower with Rapunzel's hair to see if it is tall enough.

5. Count the blocks you used to build your tower. Write the number of blocks in the box.

6. Circle one answer below:

My estimate was **LESS THAN** the number of blocks I used.

My estimate was THE SAME AS the number of blocks I used.

My estimate was **GREATER THAN** the number of blocks I used.

Name _____

A Stick Tower for Rapunzel

Directions: Use the yarn and craft sticks to complete the activities below.

1. Pretend the piece of yarn is Rapunzel's hair.

2. Estimate: How many craft sticks will it take to build a tower as tall as Rapunzel's hair? Write your guess in the box.

3. Build a tower.

4. Measure your tower with Rapunzel's hair to see if it is tall enough.

5. Count the craft sticks you used to build your tower. Write the number of craft sticks in the box.

6. Circle one answer below:

   My estimate was **LESS THAN** the number of craft sticks I used.

   My estimate was THE SAME AS the number of craft sticks I used.

   My estimate was **GREATER THAN** the number of craft sticks I used.

Name _____

A Brick Tower for Rapunzel

Directions: Use the yarn and bricks to complete the activities below.

1. Pretend the piece of yarn is Rapunzel's hair.

2. Estimate: How many bricks will it take to build a tower as tall as Rapunzel's hair? Write your guess in the box.

3. Build a tower.

4. Measure your tower with Rapunzel's hair to see if it is tall enough.

5. Count the bricks you used to build your tower. Write the number of bricks in the box.

6. Circle one answer below:

My estimate was **LESS THAN** the number of bricks I used.

My estimate was THE SAME AS the number of bricks I used.

My estimate was **GREATER THAN** the number of bricks I used.

Building in Fairy Tale Land

Differentiation Strategy

 Leveled Learning Centers

Standards

- **Science:** Students will know that different objects are made up of many different types of materials and have many different observable properties.

- **TESOL:** Students will use English to obtain, process, construct, and provide subject matter information in spoken and written form.

Materials

- lesson resources (pages 108–111)
- large construction paper
- markers
- glue
- craft supplies
- several fairy tales (*See page 167.*)
- audio recordings of fairy tales

Procedures

Preparation Note: Decide on a few materials that you would like to use for demonstration purposes. These can include craft sticks, straws, cloth, felt, chenille craft sticks, fun foam, cotton balls, wallpaper, wrapping paper, and tissue paper. Create a mini-poster for each of the materials you choose to have your students use. On the top of a sheet of construction paper, glue a sample of one material. Write the name of the material beside it. Divide the paper into two sections. Label one section *Description* and the second section *Uses*.

Set up four centers in the classroom with the craft supplies and copies of the appropriate *Building Centers* activity sheets (pages 109–110).

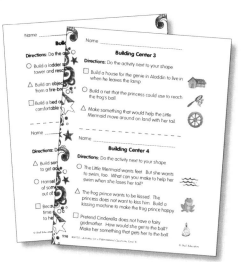

❶ Introduce each of the materials to your students by showing them the charts one at a time. Give students a sample of the material to pass around and look at. Discuss the color, size, shape, and texture of each object. Write that information on the poster. Make a list of items the material could be used to create. For example, a cotton ball is white, small, round, and soft. It could be used for a pillow or as padding to protect a person from a fall.

Building in Fairy Tale Land

2 Distribute the *Fairy Tale Comparison Chart* activity sheet (page 108) to students. Over the course of several days, read and discuss several fairy tales with the class. As you read, discuss the various objects in each fairy tale and the materials used to make those objects. Record these on the *Fairy Tale Comparison Chart*. Ask students to think about how the materials on your posters could be used to make the objects in the fairy tales. Remind students that some materials will work better for certain activities than others.

★ **English Language Support**—Provide English language learners with recordings of different fairy tales. Allow them to listen to the stories to gain a better understanding of the plot.

3 Tell students that they will get to practice building things for the characters in fairy tales at their learning centers.

4 Assign students a shape based on their readiness levels. Tell students that they will do the activity at each center that matches the shape assigned to them. Model this for the students at all of the centers.

5 Assign students to begin working at one of the four learning centers. After providing enough time for students to finish their work, have the groups rotate. Repeat this until all students have visited each of the four centers. Or, allow students to choose the centers where they want to work. Students do not need to visit all of the centers if time does not permit.

6 If students finish early, they may complete the Anchor Activity.

Assessment

Have students fill out the *Fairy Tales Building Self-Assessment* (page 111). Consider their responses along with your own observations when assigning levels in future differentiated lessons.

Activity Levels
▲
Above Grade Level
■
On Grade Level
●
Below Grade Level

Anchor Activity

Have students select a fairy tale to look at or read. Provide students with a variety of fairy tale books. When students have finished looking at the fairy tale, ask them to build an object that would be helpful in that fairy tale. Provide students an opportunity to tell about the fairy tale and explain the purpose of the object they built.

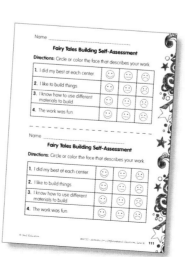

Name _____

Fairy Tale Comparison Chart

Directions: Read each fairy tale. Then, fill in the chart below.

Fairy Tale	Things in the Fairy Tales	Materials Needed to Build the Things

Name _____

Building Center 1

Directions: Do the activity next to your shape.

○ Build a ladder so the prince can climb the tower and rescue Rapunzel.

△ Build an object that would protect a princess from a fire-breathing dragon.

□ Build a bed and pillow to keep Sleeping Beauty comfortable while she sleeps.

- -

Name _____

Building Center 2

Directions: Do the activity next to your shape.

△ Build something for Hansel and Gretel to use to get across the lake.

○ Hansel and Gretel found a candy house. Think of something you like. Draw a house made out of things you like.

□ Because the frog is so small, he has a hard time getting to the princess. Make something to help the frog reach the princess.

Name _____

Building Center 3

Directions: Do the activity next to your shape.

☐ Build a house for the genie in Aladdin to live in when he leaves the lamp.

○ Build a net that the princess could use to reach the frog's ball.

△ Make something that would help the Little Mermaid move around on land with her tail.

- -

Name _____

Building Center 4

Directions: Do the activity next to your shape.

○ The Little Mermaid wants feet. But she wants to swim, too. What can you make to help her swim when she loses her tail?

△ The frog prince wants to be kissed. The princess does not want to kiss him. Build a kissing machine to make the frog prince happy.

☐ Pretend Cinderella does not have a fairy godmother. How would she get to the ball? Make her something that gets her to the ball.

Name _____

Fairy Tales Building Self-Assessment

Directions: Circle or color the face that describes your work.

1. I did my best at each center.	☺	😐	☹
2. I like to build things.	☺	😐	☹
3. I know how to use different materials to build.	☺	😐	☹
4. The work was fun.	☺	😐	☹

— —

Name _____

Fairy Tales Building Self-Assessment

Directions: Circle or color the face that describes your work.

1. I did my best at each center.	☺	😐	☹
2. I like to build things.	☺	😐	☹
3. I know how to use different materials to build.	☺	😐	☹
4. The work was fun.	☺	😐	☹

Building Maps

Differentiation Strategy

 Tiered Assignments

Standards

• **Social Studies:** Students will understand the physical and human characteristics of a place.

• **TESOL:** Students will use English to obtain, process, construct, and provide subject matter information in spoken and written form.

Materials

• lesson resources (pages 114–117)

• labeled pictures of landforms (mountains, lakes, rivers, ponds, deserts, forests, oceans, hills)

• chart paper and markers

• fairy tales (See page 167.)

• large construction paper

• crayons

Procedures

1 Show students pictures of various landforms. Ask students to identify each landform and talk about its characteristics. Discuss which landforms are seen in and around your school community. Allow students to share observations or experiences related to these different landforms. Ask students to determine whether the landforms they are talking about are near the school community or far away.

★ **English Language Support**—Provide English language learners pictures of various landforms. Label the pictures with the names of each landform.

2 Create a three-column chart on a sheet of chart paper. Label the chart *Fairy Tales*. Label the first column *Fairy Tale* and the second column *Landforms*. Leave the third column blank.

3 Over the course of several days, read and discuss several fairy tales with the class. Before reading each story, ask students to think about the landforms found in each fairy tale. Upon completing a book, write the fairy tale title on your chart. Ask students to name landforms they identified in the fairy tale. Write these landforms in the appropriate space on the chart.

4 After you have read all the fairy tales, divide the class into heterogeneous groups. There should be one group for each fairy tale that you read. Give each group a fairy tale, a large sheet of construction paper, and crayons. Ask each group to draw pictures of the landforms found in their fairy tales. Encourage students to label their pictures. When the students have completed their drawings, meet together as a whole group. Allow students to share their drawings, compare their drawings to the chart, and discuss which landforms are most common in the fairy tales.

5 Explain that the landforms listed on the chart and the landforms they drew are physical characteristics of a place. Places also have objects made by people, such as castles, cottages, or bridges. Label the third column of your chart *Man-Made Objects*. Ask students to name man-made objects in the fairy tales. List the objects that students name in the appropriate place on the chart.

Building Maps

6 Tell students that because it is difficult to draw real objects on a map, mapmakers will represent these objects with symbols. The symbols are shown on a map and in the *map key*. Distribute copies of the *Make a Map Key* activity sheet (page 114) to help students understand how to draw symbols to represent objects on their maps. You may have students complete this activity independently, with a partner, or in small groups.

7 Explain to students that they will have an opportunity to create their own fairy tale settings. Explain that they will be creating a map of a fairy tale land. Distribute copies of the *Map Of Fairy Tale Land* activity sheets (pages 115–117) to students based on their readiness levels.

Activity Levels
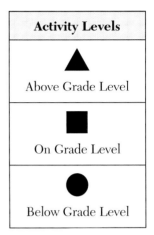
▲
Above Grade Level
■
On Grade Level
●
Below Grade Level

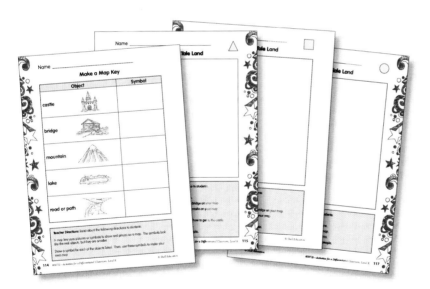

8 Review the directions with each group individually and answer any questions that students may have. Bring all of your below-grade-level students together and work with them as a group to complete their assignment.

9 If students finish early, they may complete the Anchor Activity.

Assessment

Evaluate students' assignments to determine whether the lesson objective was met. Plan mini-lessons to reteach the content to small groups of students, as necessary.

Anchor Activity

Have students build a three-dimensional model of their fairy tale land. Provide clay, craft sticks, toothpicks, construction paper, yarn, glue, scissors, and other building materials. Allow students to use other materials to create bridges, castles, towers, or other items that they can think of for their maps. Encourage students to create a map key when they complete their maps.

Name _____

Make a Map Key

Object		Symbol
castle	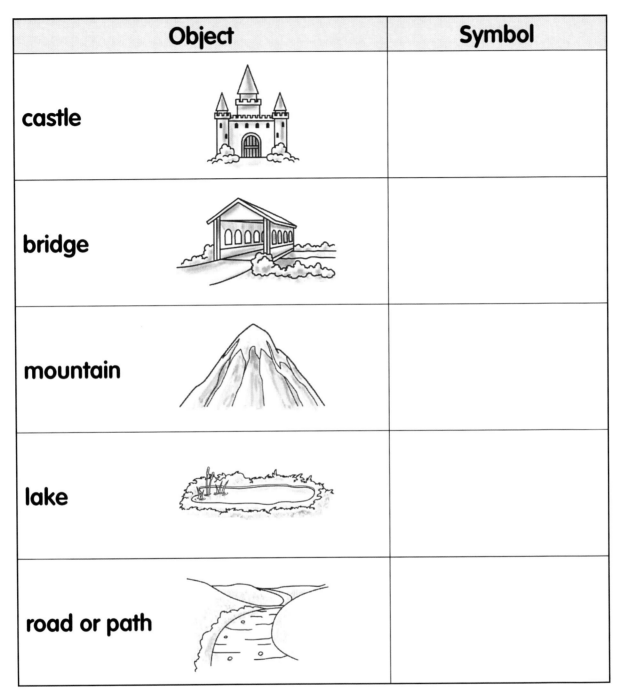	
bridge		
mountain		
lake		
road or path		

Teacher Directions: Read aloud the following directions to students:

A map key uses pictures or symbols to show real places on a map. The symbols look like the real objects, but they are smaller.

Draw a symbol for each of the objects listed. Then, use these symbols to make your own map.

Name _____

Map of Fairy Tale Land

Teacher Directions: Read aloud the following directions to students:

1. Create a map of a fairy tale land.

2. Draw symbols for at least four different landforms.

3. Draw a symbol to show where you would build a bridge on your map.

4. Draw a symbol to show where you would build a castle on your map.

5. Draw a fairy tale character on your map.

6. Draw an arrow that shows the fairy tale character how to get to the castle.

7. Use a green crayon to circle the natural landforms.

8. Use a blue crayon to circle the things made by people.

Name _____

Map of Fairy Tale Land

Directions: Read aloud the following directions to students:

1. Create a map of a fairy tale land.

2. Draw symbols for at least three different landforms.

3. Draw a symbol to show where you would build a bridge on your map.

4. Draw a symbol where you would build a castle on your map.

5. Use a green crayon to circle the natural landforms.

6. Use a blue crayon to circle the things made by people.

Name _____

Map of Fairy Tale Land

Directions: Read aloud the following directions to students:

1. Create a map of a fairy tale land.

2. Draw symbols for at least two different landforms.

3. Show where you would build a castle on your map.

4. Use a green crayon to circle the natural landforms.

5. Use a blue crayon to circle the things made by people.

Planting Writing Skills

Differentiation Strategy

 Choices Board

Standards

- **Language Arts:** Students will use writing and other methods to describe familiar persons, places, objects, or experiences.

- **TESOL:** Students will use English to obtain, process, construct, and provide subject matter information in spoken and written form.

Materials

- lesson resources (pages 120–123)
- scissors
- chart paper and markers
- crayons
- picture cards of plants
- a book about plants (*See page 167.*)
- glue
- craft sticks
- art supplies
- pocket chart (*optional*)

Procedures

Preparation Note: Make a copy of the *Plenty of Plants Choices Cards* activity sheets (pages 121–123). Cut out the cards and place them in a pocket chart or on a bulletin board. Create a *KWL* chart on chart paper with three columns labeled **Know**, **Want to Know**, and **Learned**. Display it in a prominent place in the classroom.

1 Distribute drawing paper to students. Ask them to draw pictures or write everything they know about plants.

★ **English Language Support**—Provide English language learners with labeled picture cards of words they may use in their writing. The picture cards may include a plant, a flower, water, the sun, a stem, leaves, roots, and petals. Allow English language learners to draw pictures or dictate rather than write words or sentences.

2 Allow each student to share his or her information about plants. Attach students' pictures to the *Know* section of your *KWL* chart.

3 Ask students to list things they want to know about plants. Write their ideas in the *Want to Know* section of the *KWL* chart. See if students can name ways to learn about plants. Explain that one way to learn about plants is by reading books about plants.

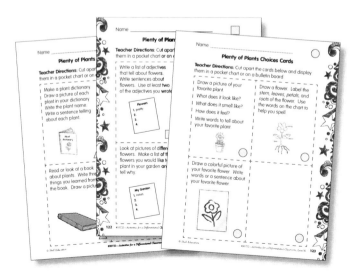

Planting Writing Skills

4 Read a book about plants to the class. Discuss the information presented in the book. Check your chart to see if the book answered any of the students' questions. Write answers to the questions in the *Learned* section of the *KWL* chart.

5 Tell students that they will have an opportunity to learn more about plants in the next activity. Assign students a shape based on their readiness levels.

6 Show students the pocket chart that has the choices board cards displayed. You may wish to use the *Plenty of Plants Choices Board* sheet (page 120) as a guide for displaying the cards. Tell students that they will choose two activities to complete that match their shape. Or, you can make copies of the *Plenty of Plants Choices Cards* activity sheets (pages 121–123) and distribute the leveled activity sheet to each student. One square is left blank so that you can create an additional activity or allow students to create their own activity.

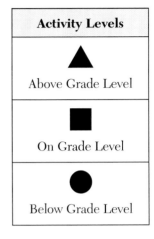

7 Distribute any necessary materials to help students complete the activities. Provide students with enough time to complete two activities or assign the activities as homework.

8 If students finish early, they may complete the Anchor Activity.

Assessment

Evaluate the activities students complete to assess whether lesson objectives were met. If necessary, prepare to reteach lessons for small groups of struggling students.

Activity Levels	
▲	Above Grade Level
■	On Grade Level
●	Below Grade Level

Anchor Activity

Have students write a book that gives information about plants. Ask students to think of the important things they learned about plants. Provide blank booklets (staple several sheets of paper together) for students to use. Have them draw a picture of what they learned in their book. Encourage students to write a sentence or words about their pictures. Give students opportunities to share their books with their classmates. Ask students to state facts they learned from the books written by their classmates.

Plenty of Plants Choices Board

Teacher Directions: Display the choices cards (pages 121–123) on a pocket chart or bulletin board as shown below:

Draw a picture of your favorite plant. What does it look like? What does it smell like? How does it feel? Write words about your favorite plant. ○	Write a list of adjectives that tell about flowers. Write sentences about flowers. Use at least two of the adjectives you wrote. □	Make a plant dictionary. Draw a picture of each plant in your dictionary. Write the plant name. Write a sentence telling about each plant. △
Read or look at a book about plants. Write three things you learned from the book. Draw a picture. △	Draw a colorful picture of your favorite flower. Write words or a sentence about your favorite flower. ○	Look at pictures of different flowers. Make a list of the flowers you would like to plant in your garden and tell why. □
Use craft sticks to make two flower puppets. If flowers could talk, what would they say? Do a puppet show for your friends. □	A *botanist* is a person who studies plants. Write a letter to a botanist. Ask the botanist questions about how to take care of plants. △	Draw a flower. Label the *stem, leaves, petals,* and *roots* of the flower. Use the words on the chart to help you spell. ○

Plenty of Plants Choices Cards

Teacher Directions: Cut apart the cards below and display them in a pocket chart or on a bulletin board.

Make a plant dictionary. Draw a picture of each plant in your dictionary. Write the plant name. Write a sentence telling about each plant.

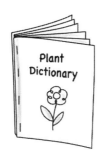

A *botanist* is a person who studies plants. Write a letter to a botanist. Ask the botanist questions about how to take care of plants.

Read or look at a book about plants. Write three things you learned from the book. Draw a picture.

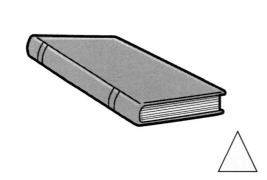

Plenty of Plants Choices Cards

Teacher Directions: Cut apart the cards below and display them in a pocket chart or on a bulletin board.

Write a list of adjectives that tell about flowers. Write sentences about flowers. Use at least two of the adjectives you wrote.

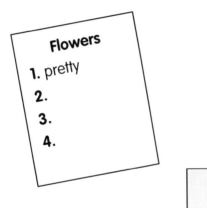

Use craft sticks to make two flower puppets. If flowers could talk, what would they say? Do a puppet show for your friends.

Look at pictures of different flowers. Make a list of the flowers you would like to plant in your garden and tell why.

Plenty of Plants Choices Cards

Teacher Directions: Cut apart the cards below and display them in a pocket chart or on a bulletin board.

Draw a picture of your favorite plant.

What does it look like?

What does it smell like?

How does it feel?

Write words to tell about your favorite plant.

Draw a flower. Label the *stem, leaves, petals,* and *roots* of the flower. Use the words on the chart to help you spell.

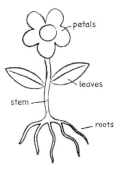

Draw a colorful picture of your favorite flower. Write words or a sentence about your favorite flower.

All Sorts of Plants

Differentiation Strategy

 Leveled Learning Centers

Standards

- **Mathematics:** Students will sort and group objects by attributes.

- **TESOL:** Students will use English to obtain, process, construct, and provide subject matter information in spoken and written form.

Materials

- lesson resources (pages 126–129)

- plant seeds

- bowls or small cups

- art supplies

- cards labeled *size, shape,* and *color*

- ice-cube trays or empty egg cartons

Procedures

Preparation Note: Determine how many groups you would like to have for the seed-sorting activity. It is recommended that you have no more than four students in each group. You will need at least four different types of seeds for each group. Place seeds in bowls or small cups so they can be easily distributed to students. Label each bowl or cup so that students will learn the names of the seeds they are sorting.

Set up three centers around the classroom. At each center, place crayons, scissors, glue, large construction paper, and copies of one of the *Sorting Flowers* center activity sheets (pages 126–128).

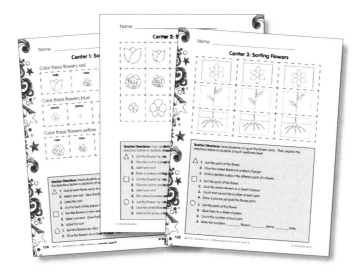

❶ Divide the class into small groups of no more than four students each. Tell students that they are going to be gardeners today and will have an opportunity to work with seeds. Ask students to name ways in which seeds could be sorted, such as by size, shape, or color. List these ways on the board.

★ **English Language Support**—Show English language learners cards labeled *size, shape,* and *color.* Talk about what *size* means and draw large and small circles on the *size* card and label each circle. On the *shape* card, draw pictures of various seed shapes and discuss those shapes. Color and label colors of the seeds on the *color* card. Allow students to use these cards as a reference during sorting activities.

All Sorts of Plants

2 Distribute the cups with seeds and a container for sorting seeds, such as an ice-cube tray or an egg carton, to each group. Tell students to work together to sort the seeds. As students are working in their groups, circulate around the room and ask students about different ways they are sorting their seeds.

3 Show students how to divide a sheet of paper by drawing lines across the paper. Allow a group to show how they sorted their seeds on the paper. Ask students to describe the attributes of the seeds in each pile. Label each section.

4 Tell students that they will have more sorting opportunities in their learning centers.

5 Assign students a shape according to their readiness levels. Tell students that they will complete the activity at each center that matches the shape assigned to them.

6 Assign students to one of the three learning centers. After giving students enough time to finish their work, have the groups rotate. Repeat this until all students have visited each of the three centers.

7 If students finish early, they may complete the Anchor Activity.

Assessment

Use the *Plants Assessment Checklist* (page 129) to assess students as they work. This checklist will allow you to record students' progress.

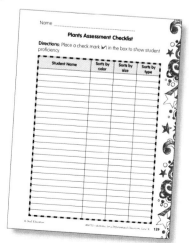

Activity Levels
▲
Above Grade Level
■
On Grade Level
●
Below Grade Level

Anchor Activity

Have students sort flowers in as many different ways as possible. Provide artificial flowers for students to sort. Have them draw pictures or write sentences telling the different ways the flowers were sorted.

Name _____

Center 1: Sorting Flowers

Color these cards red.

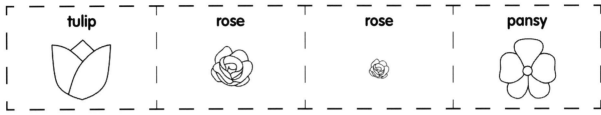

| tulip | rose | rose | pansy |

Color these cards blue.

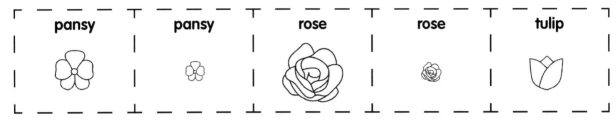

| pansy | pansy | rose | rose | tulip |

Color these cards yellow.

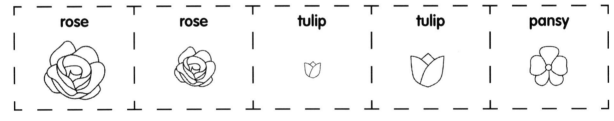

| rose | rose | tulip | tulip | pansy |

Teacher Directions: Have students color and cut apart the flower cards. Then, explain the directions below to students at each readiness level.

△ 1. Find at least three ways to sort the flowers.

   2. Select one sort. Glue the flowers to a sheet of paper.

   3. Label the sort.

   4. On the back of the paper, write about the other two sorts.

▢ 1. Sort the flowers in two ways.

   2. Select one sort. Glue the flowers to a sheet of paper.

   3. Label the sort.

◯ 1. Sort the flowers by color.

   2. Glue the flowers to a sheet of paper. Name the sort.

Name _____

Center 2: Sorting Flowers

Teacher Directions: Have students cut apart the flower cards. Then, explain the directions below to students at each readiness level.

△ 1. Sort the flowers by size.

2. Glue the sort to a sheet of paper.

3. Label your sort.

4. Write a sentence telling another way to sort these flowers.

☐ 1. Sort the flowers by size.

2. Glue the sort to a sheet of paper.

3. Label your sort.

4. Tell a friend another way you could sort these flowers.

○ 1. Sort the flowers by size.

2. Glue the sorted flowers to a sheet of paper.

3. Label the groups *small*, *medium*, or *large*.

Name _____

Center 3: Sorting Flowers

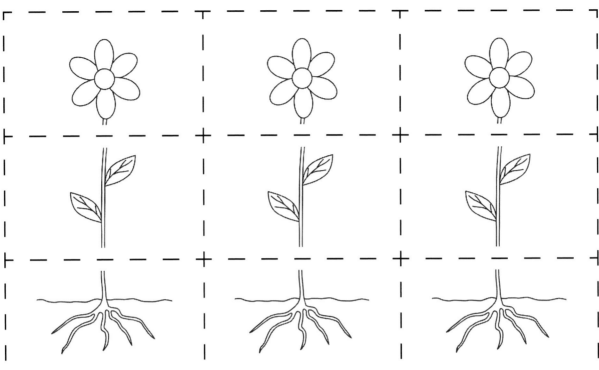

Teacher Directions: Have students cut apart the flower cards. Then, explain the directions below to students at each readiness level.

△ 1. Sort the parts of the flower.

    2. Glue the sorted flowers to a sheet of paper.

    3. Write a sentence about the different parts of a flower.

▢ 1. Sort the parts of the flower.

    2. Glue the sorted flowers to a sheet of paper.

    3. Count and record the number of each part.

    4. Draw a picture using all the flower parts.

○ 1. Sort the parts of the flower.

    2. Glue them to a sheet of paper.

    3. Count the number of each part.

    4. Write the numbers. _____ flowers, _____ stems, _____ roots

Plants Assessment Checklist

Directions: Place a check mark (✔) in the box to show student proficiency.

Student Name	Sorts by Color	Sorts by Size	Sorts by Type

Plant Needs

Differentiation Strategy

 Bloom's Taxonomy

Standards

- **Science:** Students will know the basic needs of plants.

- **TESOL:** Students will use English to obtain, process, construct, and provide subject matter information in spoken and written form.

Materials

- lesson resources (pages 132–135)
- two identical plants
- chart paper and markers
- crayons
- art supplies

Preparation Note: At least a week prior to teaching this lesson, obtain two identical plants. Place one plant in a dark closet and do not water it. Provide water and sunlight to the second plant as needed.

1 Ask students to think of things they need in order to be healthy and grow. Distribute a small piece of drawing paper to students and have them draw at least one thing that they need to grow. Encourage students to label their objects.

2 Invite students to share their drawings with the class. Have students help sort the drawings into categories such as food, shelter, fresh air, and clothing.

3 Draw a picture of a plant on chart paper. Ask for volunteers to add to the picture by drawing things that a plant needs in order to grow, such as water, sunlight, and soil. Help students label the objects they drew.

★ **English Language Support**—Draw pictures with English language learners of things plants need to grow (water, sunlight, soil, etc.). Allow students to name these objects in their native language and then write the English word for each item near the picture. Allow students to use these pictures throughout the lesson as needed.

4 Discuss items that plants need to grow and items that students need to grow. Compare the plant chart with the pictures that students drew. Help students discover items that are similar and items that are different. You may wish to use a marker to circle the items that are similar.

5 Show the class the two plants. Explain that the plants looked the same at the time you bought them. Ask students to hypothesize about why the plants look so different. Help students understand that one plant was placed in a closet with no light or water while the other plant had all its needs met.

Plant Needs

6 Divide the class into homogeneous groups. Distribute copies of the *Blooming Plants* activity sheets (pages 132–134) to each group based on their readiness levels.

Activity Levels
▲
Above Grade Level
■
On Grade Level
●
Below Grade Level

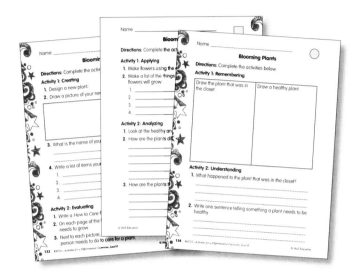

7 Meet with each group to demonstrate how to complete their activity and answer students' questions. Begin with the below-grade-level students first so they will know how to start. Monitor students as they work on assignments and provide assistance as needed.

8 If students finish early, they may complete the Anchor Activity.

Assessment

Evaluate students' work to determine whether the lesson objectives were met. Plan to reteach mini-lessons with small groups of struggling students if necessary.

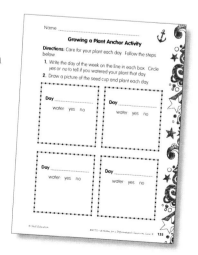

Anchor Activity

Have students plant seeds in cups. Students should write their names on craft sticks and place them in their cups. Ask students to think about what their seeds will need to grow. Have students record their plant care and its growth on the *Growing a Plant Anchor Activity* activity sheet (page 135). Materials needed include seeds, cups, soil, spoons, craft sticks, and a watering can. Students may need multiple copies of the activity sheet.

Name _____

Blooming Plants

Directions: Complete the activities below.

Activity 1: Creating

1. Design a new plant.

2. Draw a picture of your new plant.

_____

3. What is the name of your plant? What does your plant do?

    _____

    _____

4. Write a list of items your plant will need to live.

    1. _____

    2. _____

    3. _____

    4. _____

Activity 2: Evaluating

1. Write a *How to Care for Plants* book with five pages.

2. On each page of the book, draw a picture of what a plant needs to grow.

3. Next to each picture, write a sentence telling what a person needs to do to care for a plant.

Name _____

Blooming Plants

Directions: Complete the activities below.

Activity 1: Applying

1. Make flowers using the art supplies.

2. Make a list of the things you need to do to make sure flowers will grow.

1. _____

2. _____

3. _____

4. _____

Activity 2: Analyzing

1. Look at the healthy and unhealthy plants.

2. How are the plants different?

_____

_____

_____

_____

3. How are the plants the same?

_____

_____

_____

Name _____

Blooming Plants

Directions: Complete the activities below.

Activity 1: Remembering

Draw the plant that was in the closet.	Draw a healthy plant.

Activity 2: Understanding

1. What happened to the plant that was in the closet?

_____

_____

_____

2. Write one sentence telling something a plant needs to be healthy.

_____

_____

Name _____

Growing a Plant Anchor Activity

Directions: Care for your plant each day. Follow the steps below.

1. Write the day of the week on the line in each box. Circle *yes* or *no* to tell if you watered your plant that day.

2. Draw a picture of the seed cup and plant each day.

Day _____

water: yes   no

Day _____

water: yes   no

Day _____

water: yes   no

Day _____

water: yes   no

Plants Around the World

Differentiation Strategy

 Discovery Learning

Standards

- **Social Studies:** Students will understand that areas can be classified as regions according to physical criteria.

- **TESOL:** Students will use English to obtain, process, construct, and provide subject matter information in spoken and written form.

Materials

- lesson resources (pages 138–141)

- pictures of the regions to be studied (rainforest, desert, mountain, polar) (*See page 167.*)

- pictures of plants that grow in the various regions

- two identical plants

- camera

- chart paper and markers

- art supplies

- magazines or catalogs

Procedures

Preparation Note: Collect pictures of rainforests, deserts, mountains, and polar regions. In addition, collect pictures of plants that grow in the various regions. Refer to the *Regions and Plants Information* sheet (page 138) to learn types of plants that grow in each region. In addition, obtain two identical plants. Take a picture of the two plants. Place one plant in a freezer for a few days prior to the lesson. Provide regular care to the other plant.

Set up three stations in the classroom with the following materials:

- **Station 1**—the healthy plant, crayons, pencils, copies of *Pretty Plant: Station 1* (page 139)

- **Station 2**—the plant that had been in the freezer, crayons, pencils, pictures of plants that grow in the polar region, copies of *Poor Plant: Station 2* (page 140)

- **Station 3**—labeled pictures of different regions, labeled pictures of plants that grow in various regions, magazines or catalogs with pictures of plants, crayons, pencils, scissors, glue, copies of *Planting Place: Station 3* (page 141).

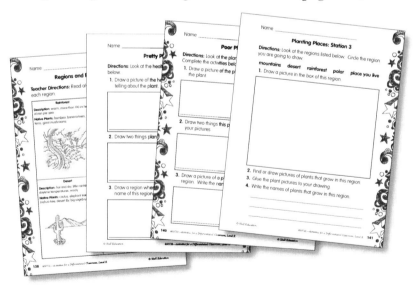

❶ Ask students to name items that a plant needs to grow. List their ideas on chart paper. Be sure students talk about seeds, soil, water, a comfortable temperature, air, and sunlight. You may wish to draw pictures of each of these on your chart.

Plants Around the World

2 Show students pictures of each region, one at a time. Discuss the characteristics of each region and the plants they see in the pictures. Explain that different plants live in different regions because the climate or weather varies. Plants that grow well in one region may not grow well in another because they are not receiving what they need to survive.

3 Display the two plants for students to see. Show students the picture of the plants before one was placed in the freezer. Allow students to hypothesize about why the plants look so different now. Explain that one plant was well cared for and the other plant was placed in a freezer. Refer to your chart of plant needs and discuss which plant had each of its needs met. Help students understand that the plants you used grow in areas that have a comfortable temperature.

4 Show students pictures of plants from different regions. Work together as a class to sort the plants according to the region in which they grow. Discuss what allows the different plants to grow successfully in their regions.

★ **English Language Support**—Provide English language learners with a chart containing pictures of the various regions (rainforest, desert, mountain, polar). Label the pictures and allow these students to refer to them during the lesson and activities.

5 Tell students that they will be learning more about plants, how they grow, and where they grow. Demonstrate and explain each of the stations to students. Allow students to select the station where they would like to work.

6 Give students enough time to complete the work at each station and then have the groups rotate. Continue to rotate until students have visited all three stations.

7 If students finish early, they may complete the Anchor Activity.

Assessment

Circulate and ask questions of students as they work at the stations. Make anecdotal notes about students' understanding to keep with their records.

Anchor Activity

Have students divide a sheet of drawing paper into four sections. Have them write the names of the regions studied in each section. Have students illustrate the regions and draw a plant that is native to that region. Encourage them to label their plant drawings. Allow students to share their pictures with classmates and compare the plants that grow in various regions.

Name _____

Regions and Plants Information

Teacher Directions: Read aloud the description of each region.

Rainforest	Mountains
Description: warm, more than 100 inches of rain per year	**Description:** warmer in the foothills, colder as you get higher; little plant life higher up
Native Plants: bamboo, banana trees, ferns, giant mushrooms	**Native Plants:** pine trees, maple trees, moss

Desert	Polar
Description: hot and dry, little rainfall, high daytime temperatures, windy	**Description:** mostly snow and ice; stays frozen most of the year; winters are long, cold, and dark; summers are warmer with lots of sunshine; trees do not grow here
Native Plants: cactus, elephant tree, Joshua tree, desert lily, big sagebrush	**Native Plants:** arctic moss, arctic willow, bearberry, arctic poppy

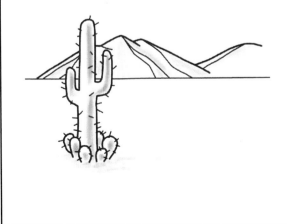

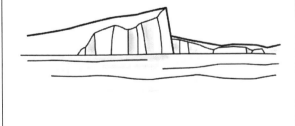

Name _____

Pretty Plant: Station 1

Directions: Look at the healthy plant. Complete the activities below.

1. Draw a picture of the healthy plant. Write a sentence telling about the plant.

```
┌─────────────────────────────────────────────┐
│                                             │
│                                             │
│                                             │
│                                             │
│  _____│
└─────────────────────────────────────────────┘
```

2. Draw two things plants need to grow. Label your pictures.

```
┌──────────────────────┬──────────────────────┐
│                      │                      │
│                      │                      │
│                      │                      │
│  _____  │  _____  │
└──────────────────────┴──────────────────────┘
```

3. Draw a region where your plant could live. Write the name of this region.

```
┌─────────────────────────────────────────────┐
│                                             │
│                                             │
│                                             │
│                                             │
│  _____│
└─────────────────────────────────────────────┘
```

Name _____

Poor Plant: Station 2

Directions: Look at the plant that has been in the freezer. Complete the activities below.

1. Draw a picture of the plant. Write a sentence telling about the plant.

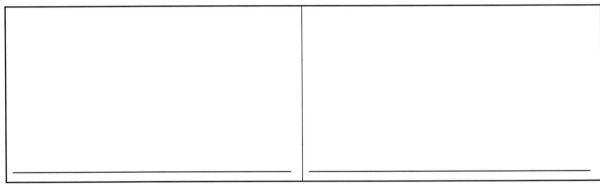

2. Draw two things this plant needed to be healthy. Label your pictures.

3. Draw a picture of a plant that could grow in a very cold region. Write the name of this plant.

Name _____

Planting Places: Station 3

Directions: Look at the regions listed below. Circle the region you are going to draw.

mountains   desert   rainforest   polar   place you live

1. Draw a picture in the box of this region.

2. Find or draw pictures of plants that grow in this region.

3. Glue the plant pictures to your drawing.

4. Write the names of plants that grow in this region.

_____

_____

_____

Animal Stories: Real and Fantasy

Differentiation Strategy

 Discovery Learning

Standards

- **Language Arts:** Students will use reading skills and strategies to understand a variety of familiar literary passages and texts.

- **TESOL:** Students will use English to obtain, process, construct, and provide subject matter information in spoken and written form.

Materials

- lesson resources (pages 144–147)

- animal books (*See page 144.*)

- 12" x 18" paper

- audio recordings of selected stories

- crayons

Procedures

Preparation Note: Fold two large sheets of 12" x 18" paper in half so that they look like books. On the cover of one, write *Fiction*. On the cover of the other, write *Nonfiction*.

Set up three stations in the classroom with the following materials:

- **Animal Clues Station**—Copies of the *Animal Clues* activity sheet (page 145); animal books; crayons

- **Drawing Conclusions Station**—Copies of the *Drawing Conclusions* activity sheet (page 146); animal books; crayons

- **Comparing Fiction and Nonfiction Books Station**—Copies of the *Comparing Fiction and Nonfiction Books* activity sheet (page 147); animal books; crayons

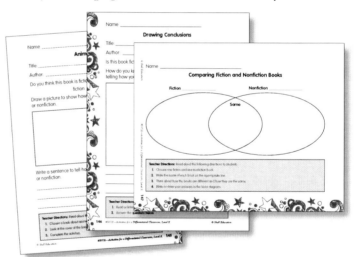

❶ Show students the "books" you created (see Preparation Note). Read the word written on each. Ask students to name characteristics they may know about fiction and nonfiction books. Write their responses inside the appropriate book. Be sure students understand fiction books are stories that are made up, and nonfiction books are stories that are true.

Animal Stories: Real and Fantasy

2 Show students a nonfiction book about animals. (Refer to the *Animal Bibliography* on page 144 for suggestions.) Read the book aloud to the class. After you have read the book, ask students if they think the book is fiction or nonfiction. Have students name clues that helped them determine that the book was nonfiction. Add these ideas to the nonfiction book you prepared. Tell students that nonfiction books provide information and help us learn about different topics.

★ **English Language Support**—Provide English language learners with audio recordings of the books that will be used during the activities.

3 Show students a fiction book about animals. Read the book aloud to the class. After you have read the book, have students decide if the book is fiction or nonfiction. Write clues that let students know that this was fiction in the fiction book you prepared. Help students understand that fiction books have animal characters participate in activities that are usually done by people, not by real animals.

4 Tell students that they will be learning more about animals in fiction and nonfiction books at their stations. Demonstrate and explain each of the stations to students. Allow students to select the station where they would like to work.

5 Give students enough time to complete the work at each station and then have the groups rotate. Continue rotating until all students have visited each station.

6 Bring the class back together and have students share what they learned about animals in fiction and nonfiction books.

7 If students finish early, they may complete the Anchor Activity.

Assessment

Evaluate students' work to determine whether the lesson objective was met.

Anchor Activity

Have students select their favorite animal and write a fiction or nonfiction book about the animal. Ahead of time, staple several sheets of blank paper together in book form. Provide time for students to share their completed books with the class.

Animal Bibliography

Teacher Directions: Use the list below of suggested books for this lesson.

Animal	Fiction	Nonfiction
Penguins	*Tacky the Penguin* by Helen Lester	*Penguins!* by Gail Gibbons
Hens	*The Little Red Hen* by Paul Galdone *Henny Penny* by Paul Galdone	*Chicks and Chickens* by Gail Gibbons *From Egg to Chicken* by Anita Ganeri
Elephants	*Elmer* by David McKee *The Story of Babar* by Jean De Brunhoff	*Face to Face with Elephants* by Dereck Joubert and Beverly Joubert *Elephants* by JoAnn Early Macken
Rabbits	*The Tale of Peter Rabbit* by Beatrix Potter *My Friend Rabbit* by Eric Rohmann	*Rabbits* by JoAnn Early Macken *Rabbits, Rabbits, and More Rabbits* by Gail Gibbons
Dogs	*The Poky Little Puppy* by Janette Sebring Lowrey and Gustaf Tenggren *Harry the Dirty Dog* by Gene Zion	*Puppies* by JoAnn Early Macken *Dogs* by Seymour Simon
Monkeys	*Curious George* by H. A. Rey *Five Little Monkeys Jumping on the Bed* by Eileen Christelow	*Apes and Monkeys* by Barbara Taylor *Monkeys* by Alice Twine
Pigs	*The Three Little Pigs* by James Marshall *The Three Little Pigs* by Steven Kellogg *If You Give a Pig a Pancake* by Laura Joffe Numeroff	*Pigs* by Gail Gibbons *Pigs* by Robin Nelson
Bears	*The Three Bears* by Byron Barton *The Three Bears* by Paul Galdone *The Three Snow Bears* by Jan Brett	*Bears: Polar Bears, Black Bears and Grizzly Bears* by Deborah Hodge *Polar Bears* by Ann O. Squire

Name _____

Animal Clues

Title: _____

Author: _____

Do you think this book is fiction or nonfiction? Circle one:

fiction   nonfiction

Draw a picture to show how you know this book is fiction or nonfiction.

Write a sentence to tell how you know this book is fiction or nonfiction.

_____

_____

_____

Teacher Directions: Read aloud the following directions to students:

1. Choose a book about animals.
2. Look at the cover of the book and take a picture walk.
3. Complete the activities.

Name _____

Drawing Conclusions

Title: _____

Author: _____

Is this book fiction (not real) or nonfiction (real)? _____

How do you know? Draw a picture and write a sentence telling how you know the book is fiction or nonfiction.

_____

_____

_____

Teacher Directions: Read the steps below aloud to students.

1. Read or listen to a book about animals.

2. Answer the questions below.

Name _____

Comparing Fiction and Nonfiction Books

Fiction

Nonfiction

Same

Teacher Directions: Read aloud the following directions to students:

1. Choose one fiction and one nonfiction book.

2. Write the name of each book on the appropriate line.

3. Think about how the books are different and how they are the same.

4. Write or draw your answers in the Venn diagram.

Perfect Pets

Differentiation Strategy

 Multiple Intelligences

Standards

- **Mathematics:** Students will collect and represent information about objects or events in simple graphs.

- **TESOL:** Students will use English to obtain, process, construct, and provide subject matter information in spoken and written form.

Materials

- lesson resources (pages 150–153)
- chart paper and markers
- sticky notes
- pictures of pets
- crayons
- scissors
- snap cubes

Procedures

1 At the top of a sheet of chart paper, write the question *Do you have a pet?* Create two columns for *Yes* and *No* answers on the chart. Distribute sticky notes to students and have them write their names on the notes. Read the question on the chart to the class. Have students place their sticky notes on the chart in the appropriate place to answer the question.

2 Ask students to look at the completed chart and make observations about the information. Ask if more students have or do not have pets. Count the number of students who said *yes*. Write that number in the column. Draw tally marks to show another representation of that number. Repeat the process for the *no* column.

3 Label another sheet of chart paper *Pets*. Ask students to name the types of pets they have at home. Write these pet types on the chart, leaving room for students to add sticky notes. When all pets have been listed, distribute sticky notes to students who have pets. Have students write their names on the sticky notes and place them near the type of pet they have.

★ **English Language Support**—Show English language learners pictures of common pets. Have them name these pets in their language and then name the pets in English. Label the pictures with the animals' English names.

4 Review the chart with the class. Have students make observations about the types of pets owned by classmates. Count the number of each pet and write it near the pet name. Have students name the most common and least common pets.

5 Write the words *Cats, Dogs,* and *Other Pets* at the top of another sheet of chart paper. Ask students to move their sticky notes from the *Pets* chart to the proper column on the *Cats, Dogs, and Other Pets* chart.

6 Tell students that they will use this information about class pet owners to complete activities. Display the charts so they are easily visible to all students.

Perfect Pets

❼ Display the *My Pets* activity sheet (page 150) for students. These activities are based on four multiple intelligences: interpersonal, visual/spatial, naturalist, and bodily/kinesthetic. Read through each activity on the sheet. Tell students they will need to select two activities to complete. Three of the activities require an additional activity sheet. Students who choose to complete the naturalist activity will need a copy of the *A Dog, a Cat, or Both?* activity sheet (page 151). Students who choose to complete the interpersonal activity will need a copy of the *Pet Questions* activity sheet (page 152). Students who choose to complete the visual/spatial activity will need a copy of the *Perfect Pet Graph activity sheet* (page 153).

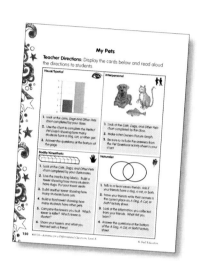

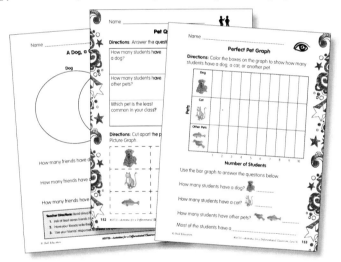

❽ Provide students with any needed materials to help them complete the activities. When students have finished their two activities, bring the class back together. Have students share their work with partners or in small groups. Walk around and observe students as they share.

❾ If students finish early, they may complete the Anchor Activity.

Assessment

Document which activities each student chose to complete and how successful he or she was. This will help in planning future differentiated activities using multiple intelligences.

Anchor Activity

Have students write their own question about pets. Have them ask their friends the question and record their responses. Provide paper so that students can create a graph or chart to display the information they gathered.

My Pets

Teacher Directions: Display the cards below and read aloud the directions to students.

Visual/Spatial

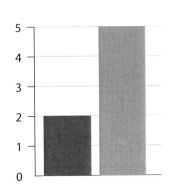

1. Look at the *Cats, Dogs and Other Pets* chart completed by your class.

2. Use the chart to complete the *Perfect Pet Graph* showing how many students have a dog, cat, or other pet.

3. Answer the questions at the bottom of the page.

Interpersonal

1. Look at the *Cats, Dogs, and Other Pets* chart completed by the class.

2. Make a Pet Owners Picture Graph.

3. Be sure to include the answers from the *Pet Questions* activity sheet in your chart.

Bodily/Kinesthetic

1. Look at the *Cats, Dogs, and Other Pets* chart completed by your classmates.

2. Use the interlocking blocks. Build a tower showing how many students have dogs. Put your tower aside.

3. Build another tower showing how many students have cats.

4. Build a third tower showing how many students have other pets.

5. Compare the towers you built. Which tower is taller? Which tower is shorter?

6. Share your towers and what you learned with a friend.

Naturalist

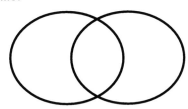

1. Talk to at least seven friends. Ask if your friends have a dog, a cat, or both.

2. Have your friends write their initials in the correct place on the *A Dog, a Cat, or Both?* activity sheet.

3. Look at the information you collected from your friends. What did you learn?

4. Answer the questions at the bottom of the *A Dog, a Cat, or Both?* activity sheet.

Name _____

A Dog, a Cat, or Both?

Dog   **Cat**

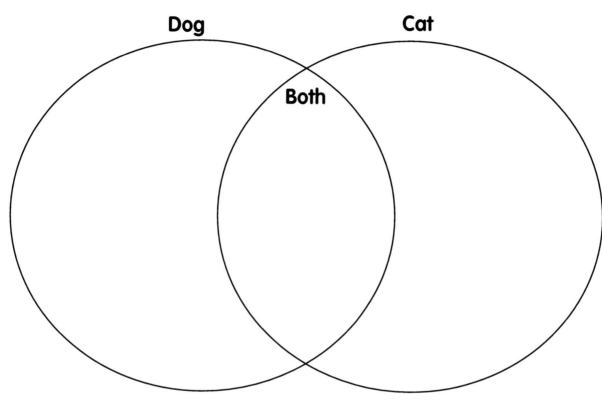

Both

How many friends have dogs? _____

How many friends have cats? _____

How many friends have a dog and cat? _____

Teacher Directions: Read aloud the following directions to students:

1. Ask at least seven friends if they have a dog, a cat, or both.

2. Have your friends write their initials in the correct place on the Venn diagram.

3. Use your friends' responses to answer the questions at the bottom of the page.

Name _____

Pet Questions

Directions: Answer the questions below.

How many students have a dog?	How many students have a cat?
How many students have other pets?	Which pet is the most common in your class?
Which pet is the least common in your class?	How many students in your class have pets?

Directions: Cut apart the pictures to make a Pet Owners Picture Graph.

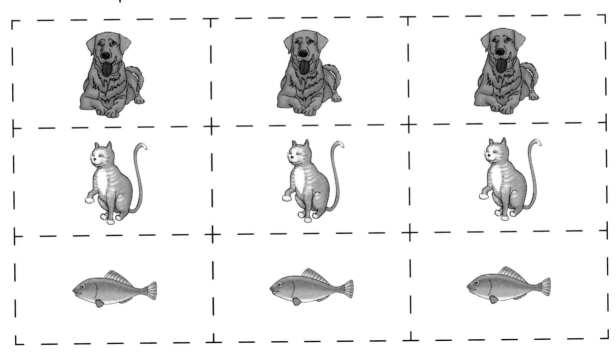

© *Shell Education*

Name _____

Perfect Pet Graph

Directions: Color the boxes on the graph to show how many students have a dog, a cat, or another pet.

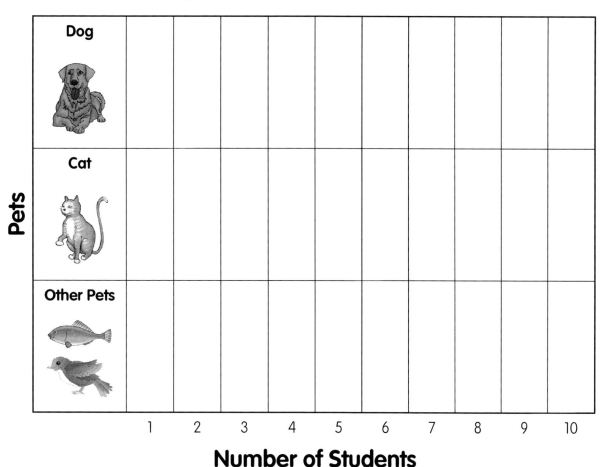

Use the bar graph to answer the questions below.

How many students have a dog?  _____

How many students have a cat?  _____

How many students have other pets?  _____

Most of the students have a _____.

Amazing Animals

Differentiation Strategy

 Choices Board

Standards

- **Science:** Students will know there are similarities and differences in the appearance and behavior of plants and animals.

- **TESOL:** Students will use English to obtain, process, construct, and provide subject matter information in spoken and written form.

Materials

- lesson resources (page 156–159)

- scissors

- chart paper and markers

- animal picture books and alphabet books *(See page 167.)*

- animal pictures (bird, bat, shark, whale, snake, lizard, lion, and tiger)

- clay or play dough

- craft sticks

- art supplies

- old magazines

- pocket chart *(optional)*

Procedures

Preparation Note: Make a copy of the *Animal Activities Choices Cards* (pages 157–159). Cut out the cards and place them in a pocket chart or on a bulletin board.

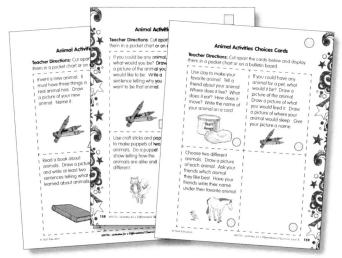

❶ Begin the lesson by asking students to name animals. Make a list of the animals that students name on a sheet of chart paper. Count the number of animals on the class list. Help students to understand that there are hundreds of different animals in the world. Some animals may seem similar, but they are also different. Explain to students that they are going to have an opportunity to carefully study animals and learn about their similarities and differences.

★ **English Language Support**—Provide English language learners with picture books about animals. An animal alphabet book would be helpful. The students can refer to the books when completing the animal activities.

❷ Display pictures of bats and birds. If you have books with information about these animals, read and discuss them with the children. Draw a Venn diagram on a large sheet of chart paper. Have students help complete the Venn diagram, comparing birds and bats. Similarities might include the facts that they fly and have wings. Differences might include sleep habits, food they eat, and appearance.

Amazing Animals

3 Divide students into six heterogeneous groups. Provide each group with an animal picture (shark, whale, snake, lizard, lion, and tiger), books about that animal, and writing paper. Ask students to make a list of facts or draw pictures about their assigned animal on the paper. Encourage students to write about where the animals live, what they look like, how they move, and what they eat.

4 Once students have completed their animal studies, allow them to share the information they learned. As a class, compare sets of animals (shark/whale, snake/lizard, lion/tiger) on Venn diagrams. Discuss the similarities and differences of each pair of animals.

5 Tell students that by using the choices board, they will have an opportunity to learn more about animals. Assign students a shape based on their readiness levels.

6 Show students the pocket chart that has the activity cards displayed. Tell students that they will choose two activities to complete that match their shape. You may wish to display the *Animal Activities Choices Board* (page 156) for students instead. Or, you can make copies of *Animal Activities Choices Board Cards* (pages 157–159) and distribute only the appropriate shape to each student. One square is left blank so that you can create an additional activity or allow students to make up their own activity.

7 Provide students with any needed materials to help them complete the activities. Give students enough time in class to complete two activities or assign the activities as weekly homework.

8 If students finish early, they may complete the Anchor Activity.

Assessment

Evaluate the activities students complete to determine whether the lesson objectives were met.

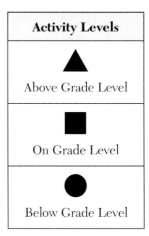

Activity Levels
▲
Above Grade Level
■
On Grade Level
●
Below Grade Level

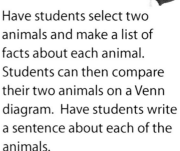

Anchor Activity

Have students select two animals and make a list of facts about each animal. Students can then compare their two animals on a Venn diagram. Have students write a sentence about each of the animals.

Animal Activities Choices Board

Teacher Directions: Display the choices cards (pages 157–159) on a pocket chart or bulletin board as shown below:

Use clay to make your favorite animal. Tell a friend about your animal. Where does it live? What does it eat? How does it move? Write the name of your animal on a card. ○	If you could be any animal, what would you be? Draw a picture of the animal you would like to be. Write a sentence telling why you want to be that animal. ☐	Invent a new animal. It must have three things a real animal has. Draw a picture of your new animal. Name it. △
Read a book about animals. Draw a picture and write at least two sentences telling what you learned about animals. △	Choose two different animals. Draw a picture of each animal. Ask your friends which animal they like best. Have your friends write their name under their favorite animal. ○	Use craft sticks and paper to make puppets of two animals. Do a puppet show telling how the animals are alike and different. ☐
Cut pictures of animals from a magazine. Make a poster of the different animals. Tell a friend about your poster. How are the animals alike and different? ☐	Choose an animal. Pretend the animal is going to a restaurant for dinner. Make a menu for the animal. What food choices will the animal have at the restaurant? △	If you could have any animal for a pet, what would it be? Draw a picture of the animal. Draw a picture of what you would feed it. Draw a picture of where your animal would sleep. Give your picture a name. ○

Animal Activities Choices Cards

Teacher Directions: Cut apart the cards below and display them in a pocket chart or on a bulletin board.

Invent a new animal. It must have three things a real animal has. Draw a picture of your new animal. Name it.

Choose an animal. Pretend the animal is going to a restaurant for dinner. Make a menu for the animal. What food choices will the animal have at the restaurant?

Read a book about animals. Draw a picture and write at least two sentences telling what you learned about animals.

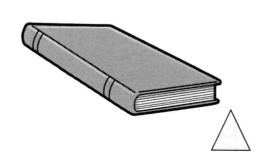

Animal Activities Choices Cards

Teacher Directions: Cut apart the cards below and display them in a pocket chart or on a bulletin board.

If you could be any animal, what would you be? Draw a picture of the animal you would like to be. Write a sentence telling why you want to be that animal.

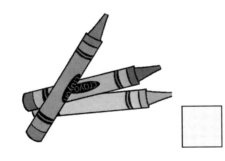

Cut pictures of animals from a magazine. Make a poster of the different animals. Tell a friend about your poster. How are the animals alike and different?

Use craft sticks and paper to make puppets of two animals. Do a puppet show telling how the animals are alike and different.

Animal Activities Choices Cards

Teacher Directions: Cut apart the cards below and display them in a pocket chart or on a bulletin board.

Use clay to make your favorite animal. Tell a friend about your animal. Where does it live? What does it eat? How does it move? Write the name of your animal on a card.

If you could have any animal for a pet, what would it be? Draw a picture of the animal. Draw a picture of what you would feed it. Draw a picture of where your animal would sleep. Give your picture a name.

Choose two different animals. Draw a picture of each animal. Ask your friends which animal they like best. Have your friends write their name under their favorite animal.

Animals All Around

Differentiation Strategy

● □ ▲ **Leveled Learning Centers**

Standards

• **Social Studies:** Students will know that places can be defined in terms of their predominant human and physical characteristics.

• **TESOL:** Students will use English to obtain, process, construct, and provide subject matter information in spoken and written form.

Materials

• lesson resources (pages 162–165)

• construction paper

• scissors

• glue

• pictures of landforms and regions

• art supplies

• magazines with photos of animals

• animal books

Procedures

Preparation Note: Create charts showing the different landforms and regions. Use construction paper to cut out a brown circle to make a cave; a long, wavy blue river; a round blue lake; a turquoise ocean; brown triangular mountains; a white polar area; a yellow desert area; a dark-green rainforest area, and a light-green grassland area. Label each of your charts.

★ **English Language Support**—Provide students with pictures of the landforms and regions that they will study. Discuss the characteristics of each picture. Name the landform or region and label the pictures. Allow students to refer to the pictures during the lesson.

1 Tell students that the world is made up of different landforms (caves, rivers, lakes, oceans, mountains) and regions (polar, desert, rainforest, and grasslands). Ask students to name regions or landforms that they know. Display the landform charts that students name. Display the remaining charts and have students help identify each landform and region.

2 Ask students to name animals that make their homes in each of the landforms and regions. Write each animal name on the appropriate chart. When working with the rainforest chart, introduce the different rainforest layers (forest floor, understory, canopy, and emergent layers). Discuss the animals that live in each area:

Rainforest Layers and Animals Chart

Forest Floor	Understory	Canopy	Emergent Layers
giant anteaters	snakes	butterflies	hummingbirds
beetles	frogs	parrots	eagles
frogs	insects	toucans	bats
lizards	bats	slow-moving sloth	monkeys
snakes	jaguars	tree frogs	
insects	leopards	jaguars	
	sloths	leopards	

3 Allow each student to select a region. Provide students with a sheet of paper and have them draw a picture of the landform or region they selected. When drawings are complete, have students trade their papers with a friend. Students should then draw an animal that lives in that landform or region. Encourage students to label their drawings.

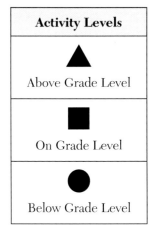

Animals All Around

4 Meet as a whole group. Allow students to share their work. Discuss the different landforms and regions and the animals that live there. Talk about how animals are able to adapt to each area in which they live.

5 Tell students that they will have more opportunities to study animals and their environments at the learning centers. Place the activity sheets *Animal Homes* (page 162), *Mixed-Up Animals* (pages 163–164), and *Animals Living in the Rainforest* (page 165) at the different learning centers.

Activity Levels
▲
Above Grade Level
■
On Grade Level
●
Below Grade Level

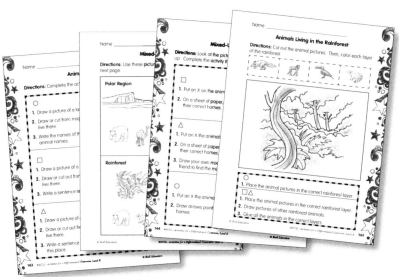

6 Assign students a shape according to their readiness levels. Tell students that they will complete the activity at each center that matches the shape assigned to them.

7 Provide students with any needed materials to help them complete the activities. Assign students to one of the three learning centers. After giving students enough time to finish their work, have the groups rotate. Repeat until all students have visited each of the three centers.

8 If students finish early, they may complete the Anchor Activity.

Assessment

Circulate around the room and observe students as they work in centers. Keep anecdotal records of students' progress.

Anchor Activity

Have students draw a picture of a landform or a region. Next, have them list all the animals that might live there. They can draw some of these animals in their picture. Have students select one of the animals and write a description of that animal.

Name _____

Animal Homes

Directions: Complete the activity that matches your shape.

1. Draw a picture of a landform or region.

2. Draw or cut from magazines at least two animals that live there.

3. Write the names of the landform or region and the animal names.

1. Draw a picture of a landform or region.

2. Draw or cut out from magazines three animals that live there.

3. Write a sentence telling why it is a good animal home.

1. Draw a picture of a landform or region.

2. Draw or cut out from magazines four animals that live there.

3. Write a sentence telling why the animals live in this place.

Name _____

Mixed-Up Animals

Directions: Use these pictures to answer the questions on the next page.

Mixed-Up Animals *(cont.)*

Directions: Look at the pictures. The animals are all mixed up. Complete the activity that matches your shape.

1. Put an X on the animals that are in the wrong home.

2. On a sheet of paper, draw a picture of the animals in their correct homes.

△

1. Put an X the animals that are in the wrong home.

2. On a sheet of paper, draw a picture of the animals in their correct homes.

3. Draw your own mixed-up picture and then ask a friend to find the mistakes.

○

1. Put an X the animals that are in the wrong home.

2. Draw arrows pointing the animals to their correct homes.

Name _____

Animals Living in the Rainforest

Directions: Cut out the animal pictures. Then, color each layer of the rainforest.

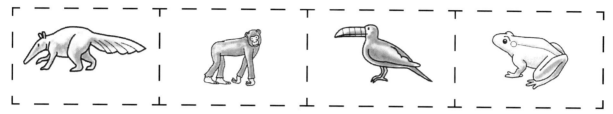

1. Place the animal pictures in the correct rainforest layer.

1. Place the animal pictures in the correct rainforest layer.

2. Draw pictures of other rainforest animals.

3. Glue all the animals in the correct layers.

References

Anderson, L. W., and D. R. Krathwohl, eds. 2001. *A taxonomy for learning, teaching, and assessing: A revision of Bloom's taxonomy of educational objectives.* Boston: Allyn and Bacon.

Bess, J. 1997. *Teaching well and liking it: Motivating faculty to teach effectively.* Baltimore, MD: Johns Hopkins University Press.

Bloom, B. S. and D. R. Krathwohl. 1984. *Taxonomy of educational objectives: Handbook I; Cognitive Domain.* White Plains, NY: Longman.

Brandt, R. 1998. *Powerful learning.* Alexandria, VA: Association for Supervision and Curriculum Development.

Bruner, J. 2004. *Toward a theory of instruction.* Cambridge, MA: Belnap Press of Harvard University Press.

Costa, A. L., and R. Marzano. 1987. Teaching the language of thinking. *Educational Leadership* 45: 29–33.

Gardner, H. 1983. *Frames of mind: The theory of multiple intelligences.* New York: Basic Books.

———. 1999. *Intelligence reframed: Multiple intelligences for the 21st Century.* New York: Basic Books.

Jensen, E. 1998. *Teaching with the brain in mind.* Alexandria, VA: Association for Supervision and Curriculum Development.

Kaplan, S. N. 2001. Layering differentiated curriculum for the gifted and talented. In *Methods and materials for teaching the gifted*, ed. F. Karnes and S. Bean, 133–158. Waco, TX: Prufrock Press.

Olsen, K. D. 1995. *Science continuum of concepts: For grades K–6.* Black Diamond, WA: Books for Educators.

Sprenger, M. 1999. *Learning and memory: The brain in action.* Alexandria, VA: Association for Supervision and Curriculum Development.

Teele, S. 1994. Redesigning the educational system to enable all students to succeed. PhD diss., University of California, Riverside.

Winebrenner, S. 1992. *Teaching gifted kids in the regular classroom.* Minneapolis, MN: Free Spirit Publishing.

Additional Resources

Where books and websites are referenced in lesson materials lists, some suggestions for these resources are provided below. Shell Education does not control the content of these websites, or guarantee their ongoing availability or links contained therein. We encourage teachers to preview these websites before directing students to use them.

Page 40—Super School Citizens

Serrano, John. *Being a Good Citizen*. Pelham, NY: Newmark Learning, 2010.

Page 76—Shaping Up My Community

Cooper, Sharon. *Whose Hat Is This? A Look at Hats Workers Wear—Hard, Tall, and Shiny*. Mankato, MN: Picture Window Books, 2007.

Kalman, Bobbie. *Community Helpers from A to Z*. New York: Crabtree Publishing, 1997.

Treays, Rebecca. *My Town*. Tulsa, OK: Educational Development Corporation, 1998.

Page 88—Community Goods and Services

Kalman, Bobbie. *Helpers in My Community*. New York: Crabtree Publishing, 2010.

Pages 100, 106, 112—Building Towers, Building in Fairy Tale Land, Building Maps

Gustafson, Scott. *Classic Fairy Tales*. Seymour, CT: Greenwich Workshop Press, 2003.

Scoggins, Liz. *The Fairy Tale Book*. New York: Scholastic Nonfiction, 2010.
(Note: Includes *Rapunzel*)

Zalinsky, Paul O. *Rapunzel*. New York: Dutton Juvenile, 1997.

Page 118—Planting Writing Skills

Fowler, Allan. *From Seed to Plant*. Danbury, CT: Children's Press, 2001.

Gibbons, Gail. *From Seed to Plant*. New York: Holiday House, 1993.

Jordan, Helene J. *How a Seed Grows*. New York: Collins, 1992.

Page 136—Plants Around the World

http://beyondpenguins.nsdl.org
http://discovermagazine.com
http://www.nationalgeographic.com

Page 154—Amazing Animals

Arlon, Penelope. *First Animal Encyclopedia*. New York: DK Publishing, 2004.

McGhee, Karen and George McKay. PhD. *National Geographic Encyclopedia of Animals*. Des Moines, IA: National Geographic Children's Books, 2006.

Smith, R. M. *An A to Z Walk in the Park*. Alexandria, VA: Clarence-Henry Books, 2008.

http://kids.nationalgeographic.com/kids

Contents of the Teacher Resource CD

Lesson Resource Pages

Page	Lesson	Filename
24–27	Letters Tell About Me	pg024.pdf
30–33	Numbers All Around Me	pg030.pdf
36–39	Friends Around Me	pg036.pdf
42–45	Super School Citizens	pg042.pdf
48–51	Popping into Descriptive Words	pg048.pdf
54–57	Sense Patterns	pg054.pdf
60–63	Making Sense of Changes	pg060.pdf
66–69	Sensing My World	pg066.pdf
72–75	People, Places, and Things in My Community	pg072.pdf
78–81	Shaping Up My Community	pg078.pdf
84–87	Tools in the Community	pg084.pdf
90–93	Community Goods and Services	pg090.pdf
96–99	Building Stories	pg096.pdf
102–105	Building Towers	pg102.pdf
108–111	Building in Fairy Tale Land	pg108.pdf
114–117	Building Maps	pg114.pdf
120–123	Planting Writing Skills	pg120.pdf
126–129	All Sorts of Plants	pg126.pdf
132–135	Plant Needs	pg132.pdf
138–141	Plants Around the World	pg138.pdf
144–147	Animal Stories: Real and Fantasy	pg144.pdf
150–153	Perfect Pets	pg150.pdf
156–159	Amazing Animals	pg156.pdf
162–165	Animals All Around	pg162.pdf

Teacher Resources

Title	Filename
Answer Key	answers.pdf
Bar Graph	bargraph.pdf
T-Chart	tchart.pdf
Three Column Chart	threecolumn.pdf
Time Line	timeline.pdf
Venn Diagram	venn.pdf